J. Anne Helgren

Rex Cats

Everything About Purchase, Care, Nutrition, Behavior, and Housing

Filled with Full-color Photographs

Illustrations by Michele Earle-Bridges

BARRON'S

2 CONTENTS

WHAT IS A REX CAT?

"What's that? It looks like a space alien!"
Rex breeds, with their short, curly
fur and unique body types, provoke such
exclamations from folks new to these
unique breeds.

What Is a Rex?

While Rex cats might look like something beamed down from the mother ship, Rex are card-carrying members of *Felis catus*, the domestic cat. What makes Rex unique are their characteristic coat mutations that make the fur curly and wavy and their agreeable, affectionate, outgoing personalities.

How do you identify a Rex cat? That depends upon how you define this unique variety. Rex cats get their name from the Rex rabbit, which possesses a coat mutation that causes individual hairs to curl, kink, wave, or be absent altogether. The Cornish Rex, Devon Rex, Selkirk Rex, and LaPerm all fall within the Rex classification, and these cats are covered in this book. By the time you finish reading this book, you will be an expert in Rex identification and, I hope, will have fallen in love with these special cats and their curly coats.

Cornish Rex have been compared to pixies, elves, and aliens from space for their satellite-dish ears, large "window-to-the-soul" eyes, and ethereal appearance.

My First Rex

My love of the Rex breeds began with a special meeting between me and a very special Rex. Buddy, a Cornish, belonged to a close friend. Over time, as I got to know this mischievous, sweet Cornish, Buddy became a close friend, too. Active, affectionate, and devoted, Buddy was the archetypal Rex, and he introduced me to the unique nature of the Rex breeds.

Buddy was remarkable in several ways. First of all, he was the most active, intelligent, inquisitive cat I have ever met. When I came to visit, instead of running under the bed like my own cats were apt to do, he would fly around the corner in eager anticipation, huge ears cocked, big eyes wide, long, whippy tail lashing with excitement. I quickly learned that no matter where I put my purse, Buddy would find it, bury his head into its recesses, and dash off with something I really didn't want to part with. This was his game, his way of gaining attention, but also, I soon realized, his way of trying to assure my return. He always led Carrie and me on a merry chase as he raced to drop the stolen item into his water dish or bat it under the refrigerator. He parted with my things only with the greatest reluctance. Soon I learned to bring with me a cat toy, an old sock (he loved my old socks), a ball—anything well perfumed with my scent and that I could leave behind. Then he was happy and left the rest of my belongings alone.

Buddy has since gone onto the Rainbow Bridge to wait for Carrie to join him. I would have sent one of my old socks with him if I could. This book is a modest tribute to Buddy and all the entertaining, lovable Rex that have brightened the world. They have brightened my life, and they will brighten yours, too.

Mutation

Mother Nature works her evolutionary magic by mutation, and it's mutation that has given us the Rex breeds. A gene at a particular place or locus on the chromosome may have more than one form because genes occasionally mutate into alternate forms. The existence of these alternate forms allows for the immense variety of variation in color, coat, and body conformation in our feline friends.

Some mutations have positive effects. For example, the mutation that created the tabby pattern benefitted the survival of the species because the protective camouflaging helped the cat blend in with its environment. Other mutations can have negative effects, such as the Scottish Fold gene, which can cause crippling bone disorders.

If the mutation is harmful enough that the offspring don't survive long enough to reproduce, the mutation dies out and doesn't affect the cat gene pool. However, some mutations continue to be passed on to subsequent generations because, while they may not be particularly helpful, they do not significantly reduce the cat's chances of survival. Other genes survive because they are recessive. It takes two copies of a recessive gene for the trait to express itself, and the gene can be carried for many generations without any effect (and without anyone knowing it's there), until paired with another copy of the gene. At that point the gene will express itself, for good or ill, in the cat's physical appearance.

Still other mutations survive because humans notice the mutations and selectively breed the cats to perpetuate the new traits and therefore create a new breed. While spontaneous mutation has given us some of our most fascinating breeds (the Rex breeds, for example), care must be taken in perpetuating natural mutations. Not every genetic change is worth keeping, because some mutations have a negative impact on the cat's health or ability to survive. That's why cat fanciers should consider carefully before undertaking the creation of a new breed.

The Rex Mutations

Mutations that affect the feline coat include plush, curly hair (the Selkirk Rex), long curly locks (the LaPerm longhair), and ultrashort wavy hair (the Cornish and Devon Rex). Other coat mutations include stiff, wiry hair (the American Wirehair) and an almost total lack of hair (the Sphynx). All of these coat types arose spontaneously and separately within the domestic cat gene pool. While the breeds have certainly been refined by human breeding programs, Mother Nature first brought these breeds to us.

Ordinary cats have three hair types—guard, awn, and down. The guard hairs, which are the least numerous of the three types, are long and stiff. They cover the top layer of the cat's coat. The guard hairs help keep the cat dry by protecting the downy underlying hairs. These hairs also have attached arrector pili muscles that contract when the cat is cold, allowing the hairs to stand up and provide more insulation. These muscles also allow the fur to fluff up when the cat is frightened or angry, to give the illusion of size, one of the cat's natural defenses.

The down and awn hairs are called the secondary hairs or the undercoat. They are more numerous than the protective guard hairs. The awn hairs are thin and usually have stiff pointed ends. The baby-fine down hairs have a very soft texture. The down is the most numerous of the hairs. It also develops mats—small, dense tangles of fur—most easily.

Rex cats, however, are different because they possess mutated genes that give these breeds their distinctive coats. Some of these mutations are dominant, and some are recessive. The Rex coats of both the Cornish and the Devon are governed by recessive genes. The two genes (respectively Rex gene I and Rex gene II) create similar—but not identical—changes in the coat. This is not as much of a coincidence as it seems. Rex mutations have been seen in many species, including rabbits, mice, horses, and other animals both wild and domestic. The Rex gene seems to be linked to the body type as well.

The Cornish Rex's coat completely lacks the long guard hairs that protect a normal cat's coat. The soft awn hairs make up the Cornish coat and form a tight, uniform wave that lies close to the body.

The Devon's Rex gene produces tight rows of curls. However, unlike the Cornish, the Devon has all three hair types, but the guard hairs are fragile and stunted.

Both the LaPerm and the Selkirk Rex's coats are governed by dominant genes. The LaPerm's genetic mutation causes the soft, silky hair to curl. This breed has all three hair types. Since the hair is silky, it doesn't have a dense, wooly feeling. Coat length varies (both longhaired and shorthaired varieties exist). On the long-hair, the curls are loose and bouncy, resembling a shag hairdo.

The Selkirk Rex's coat is curly, soft, and plush. The Selkirk possesses all three hair types. All are curly, with the curl more pronounced around the neck and tail. Even the whiskers are curly, which gives the face a whimsical appearance. Like the LaPerm, the Selkirk comes in both shorthaired and longhaired varieties.

Considerable difference exists between the longhaired and shorthaired versions of both the Selkirk and the LaPerm. The coat of the shorthaired Selkirk is plush, medium in length, and curls over the entire body. In the longhair, the dense, semilong coat hangs in loose individual ringlets and has a more dramatic look. The curls are particularly prominent around the neck and on the tail. In both hair lengths, the fur is soft and dense.

Frequently Asked Questions About Rex Cats

Q. Why are these cats called Rex?
A. They are no relation to *Jurassic Park's Tyrannosaurus rex*. Rex breeds are named after the Rex rabbit, which also has a short, wavy coat. Rex in Latin means "one holding the

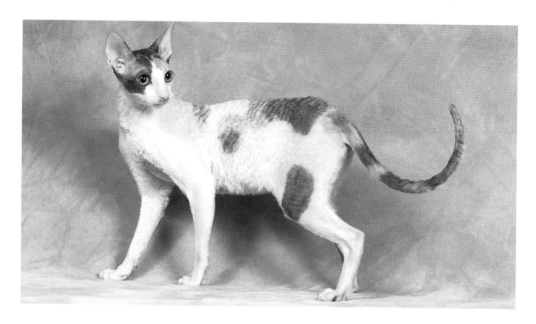

Above: Don't let the slender, willowy form fool you—the Cornish Rex is no weakling.
Below: Tortoiseshell Devon Rex. The Devon Rex's curly hair is governed by a recessive gene.
Right: The Selkirk Rex longhair.

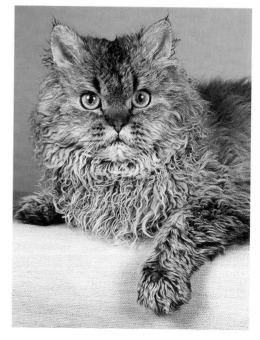

Left: A pair of Bicolor Cornish Rex kittens.
Below left: Shorthaired Chocolate Lynx Point LaPerm. The LaPerm's curls are governed by a dominant gene, which means only one parent must possess the gene for the curls to be passed on to the offspring.
Below right: While not as vocal as Siamese, Cornish Rex do speak up when they have something to say.

station in life of regent or king." As the story goes, rabbits with curly hair were first dubbed Rex in the 1890s, when King Albert of Belgium entered some of his unusual curly-haired rabbits into show competition. Rather than disqualify the king's entries and possibly anger the king, since his rabbits didn't meet the breed standard, the show officials changed the king's entry labels to read Rex. Thus a new breed of rabbit was born. All subsequent curly-haired rabbits were called by the new name.

Even though the word Rex is not included in the name of the LaPerm, it is recognized as a Rex variety.

Q. How long do Rex cats live?

A. They have the same life span as the average cat—about 10 to 15 years if kept indoors, sometimes longer.

Q. Do breeders do anything to the fur to make it curl?

A. No. Rex cats have naturally curly or wavy hair. The cats you see in the shows have not been trimmed, shaved, permed, curled, or dyed in any way.

Q. I have heard that Rex cats are hypoallergenic. Can I have one even though I'm allergic to cats?

A. Unfortunately, this widely circulated rumor is just that—a rumor. If you are allergic to cats, you will be allergic to Rex cats, too. Rex do shed less than cats with ordinary hair, which is great for keeping fur off your favorite furniture. However, cat hair is not what causes allergic reactions in humans. Rather, they are caused by an allergenic protein called Fel d1 secreted via saliva and the sebaceous glands.

When cats groom, they spread this protein onto their fur, whether it's straight, curly, wavy, or absent altogether. Rex produce just as much of this enzyme as any other cat.

However, Rex cats—particularly the Cornish and the Devon—shed less because they have less hair. So they deposit less allergen-laced hair around the house. Some allergists make several recommendations. Make the bedroom completely off limits to the cat so that you can have eight hours of allergen-free sleep. Put a good-quality, high-efficiency particulate-arresting (HEPA) air purifier into each room to filter out flakes of the enzyme that dry and become airborne. Bathe the Rex each week to remove the offending enzyme. Wipe the cat down with distilled water each day. This can help the situation, but it might not, too. It depends upon a number of factors, including the severity of the allergies. If you are allergic, plan to spend some up-close and personal time with the Rex you're considering before agreeing to buy. Since cat allergies are so common, research is ongoing and other options are in the works.

Q: Do Rex cats shed?

A: Like all cats, Rex shed. However, depending upon the breed, they do not shed as much as cats with normal hair. Devon Rex and Cornish Rex shed the least. They cannot shed hair they do not have, and Devon and Cornish Rex cats simply have less hair than most cats. Selkirks shed just like any ordinary cat and do require grooming, although their fur does not mat as easily as one might expect. LaPerms have very few guard hairs, so they shed less than cats with normal hair. LaPerms do go through molting periods where they lose much of their hair.

Unlike other breeds that shed most heavily in the fall and spring, LaPerms molt during periods of hormonal activity, such as puberty and gestation. This is a normal function of the coat, particularly with cats that are not altered. Generally, altering stops the molting.

Q: Do Rex cats need grooming?

A: Some of the Rex cats like the Devon and the Cornish have very short hair and require minimal grooming. These Rex may need regular bathing, however, because of the collection of oils on the skin. Unfortunately, with their wash-and-wear coats, they dry quickly and easily. Bathing is not too much of a chore if you train the cat to tolerate it when she is young. The LaPerm and the Selkirk require more grooming, but their grooming needs are still less than average (see page 77).

Q: Are Rex cats fragile or sickly?

A: Even though some of the Rex breeds, like the Cornish, may appear delicate because of their sleek styling, Rex are not the sissies of the cat fancy. They are muscular and athletic, not fragile—fine boned, not frail. Rex are sturdy, strong, and generally healthy. Pick one up; you will notice that it feels heavy for its size. Some lines are prone to gingivitis and a heart condition called cardiomyopathy, but this is true of many other purebreds, and mixed-breed cats, for that matter. Purebreds are often viewed as less healthy than mixed-breed cats. In some cases, it is true. Also true, however, is that tracking inheritable diseases and conditions is easier in purebreds because they have a documented family history that does not exist in mixed-breed cats.

Q. What are the differences between the Cornish and the Devon Rex?

A. Although they share similarities and both originated in southwest England, the Cornish and Devon possess two distinctly different coat mutations. The Cornish Rex completely lacks guard hairs. The soft awn hairs make up the Cornish coat and form a tight, uniform wave that lies close to the body. The Devon has all three hair types. However, the guard hairs are typically fragile and stunted, and the whisker hairs are often missing altogether. The two breeds have very different body and head types as well. When bred together, the two breeds always produce straight-haired offspring.

Q. How long do Rex cats live?

A. They have the same life span as the average domestic cat. With good care and a protected environment, they live about 15 years, sometimes longer.

A Word About Pronouns

Many cat lovers feel that the neuter pronoun "it" is not appropriate when applied to our feline friends. Therefore, in this book, you'll notice that the chapters alternate between a female cat named Callie and a male cat named Curly. This is to avoid the clumsy use of "he or she" when referring to cats, since the English language doesn't have a gender-neutral pronoun that can be used to refer to cats—and to humans, for that matter. This technique is designed to show that no sexism is intended, and to support Barron's goal to avoid sexist language in our books.

Just because cats have deigned to share their lives with humans does not mean they have lost the 35 million years of evolutionary adaptation that has made the cat what it is today. Cats are among the most successful predators this world has ever known, and the kitty purring happily in your lap is no exception.

Evolution

Most cat species share similar traits, and the domestic cat's wild origins affect its behavior today. In many ways, it is still a wild cat in domestic cat clothing.

Although the cat's journey to its present form began around 35 million years ago, the earliest known true cat is called *Proailurus*, a predator of about 20 pounds that lived during the Oligocene around 25 million years ago. *Proailurus* probably hunted small mammals but spent about half its time up in trees, taking refuge from the larger ground-dwelling predators. Eventually, *Proailurus* became extinct. However, before it did, a species called *Pseudaelurus* split from its evolutionary line. *Pseudaelurus* lived in the early Miocene about 20 million years ago. After myriad millennia, *Pseudaelurus*, too, became extinct, but not before two separate branches grew from this

Bicolor Cornish Rex. Big ears and big eyes, as well as a short curly coat, characterize this breed.

family tree. One branch developed into cats with bigger teeth, including the saber-toothed cats. None of the cats from this branch exist today, although some saber-toothed cats like *Smilodon fatalis* were still around as recently as 10,000 years ago.

The other branch of the cat family tree, however, was more successful at adapting. From this branch came our 38 modern-day cat species. In the late Miocene (10 million years ago, give or take), the modern-day cats began to evolve. In this feline branch, the canine teeth became smaller, but the cats became smarter and faster. Adaptability has always been one of the cat's most beneficial abilities and has allowed them to survive environmental changes.

One remarkable thing about the cat's evolution is that *Proailurus,* the cat family's first true ancestor, was in many basic ways very much like our modern-day cat species. In 25 million years of evolution, other animals (including the human one) have evolved to the point where their ancestors look little or

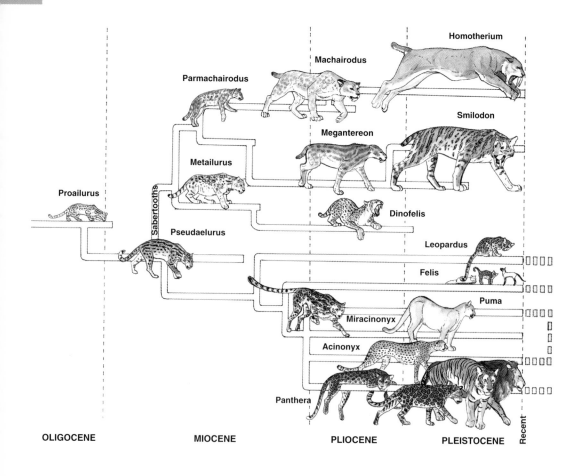

Homotherium
Machairodus
Parmachairodus
Smilodon
Meganteron
Metailurus
Dinofelis
Proailurus
Sabertooths
Leopardus
Pseudaelurus
Felis
Puma
Miracinonyx
Acinonyx
Panthera

OLIGOCENE   MIOCENE   PLIOCENE   PLEISTOCENE   Recent

nothing like the modern version. That happened because the evolutionary changes were necessary for survival as the climates, wildlife, and vegetation around them transformed. With cats, however, the basic structure has not changed in 25 million years. Why? Because the basic blueprint—fang and claw, flexible backbone, muscular strength—was an effective design. Cats, even 25 million years ago, were efficient hunters. As a family, they were able to survive the changes each epoch brought.

Through modern DNA testing and analysis, scientists have substantially changed their theories about how the cat family developed. The first true cat is now thought to be **Proailurus.**

That is the reason a study of the cat's ancestors and modern-day relatives teaches us so much about the behavior of our domestic cats; under the skin, they are all very similar.

The Domestic Cat's Origins

The domestic cat most likely arose from the species *Felis silvestris*, in particular the subspecies African wildcat *Felis silvestris libyca* (also spelled *lybica*). If put side to side, you might have a difficult time distinguishing the African wildcat from your domestic house cat. The African wildcat does have differences, but they are hard to spot unless you are an expert in such things. The African wildcat is slightly larger, but to the layperson it looks like a slightly larger domestic cat. Although native to Africa, Western Asia, Scotland, and Southern Europe, the African wildcat has the same structure and number of chromosomes as the domestic cat.

Domestication

When humans moved from being hunter-gatherers to being members of settled communities around 10,000 years ago, cats may have learned that humans provided a reliable food source—the vermin attracted to the food supplies. In effect, these cats exploited a newly formed ecological niche, as did the mice and rats that learned humans provided large tasty stores of food around their settlements. For a time (estimated to be between 9,000 and 4,000 years ago), cats lived in a semidomestic state, eating the vermin around and in human settlements without really becoming domestic animals in the true sense of the word.

After the process of domestication began, humans started to see cats as much more than slinking, wary, nocturnal animals. Humans learned that felines were invaluable in controlling the rodent populations that destroyed their crops and food supplies. This realization occurred around the same time that cats discovered how handy humans were in attracting tasty rodents.

The History of the Cat Fancy

The term *cat fancy* has become the common term used to describe the group of people interested in and involved with showing or breeding domestic cats. For the newcomer, the North American cat fancy can be perplexing because unlike the dog fancy, where only one main association exists—the AKC—the cat fancy has many associations from which to choose. While all have the same basic goals, the rules, regulations, and philosophies differ, sometimes greatly, from association to association. Even if you will not be showing your Rex, a basic understanding of how the cat fancy began and how today's associations operate will help you navigate the often confusing world of purebred cats.

–DID YOU KNOW?–

Cats were one of the last animals to be domesticated. That explains why they retain many of their natural behaviors and instincts. Cats have been "tamed" for only a few thousand years and have always accepted our domination with reservations. The cat has kept its self-confidence and strong, spirited personality. That is one reason humans respond to them so strongly in both positive and negative ways.

Top right: White Devon Rex.
Top left: Longhaired Tortoiseshell Selkirk Rex.
Above: Cornish Rex. The first Cornish was born
on July 21, 1950 in Cornwall, England.
Left: Shorthaired Chocolate lynx point LaPerm.

Top Left: Two Shorthaired Shaded Silver Selkirk Rex.
Above: Shorthaired Tortie and White Van Selkirk Rex. The Van pattern is characterized by patches of color on the head and tail.
Below: Longhaired blue-cream Selkirk Rex.
Left: The Selkirk is a relative newcomer to the cat fancy.

British Beginnings

Although cats and humans have had a close relationship for thousands of years, not until the mid-1800s in Britain did people began taking an interest in showing their cats and entering them into competition. At that time, cat organizations and governing bodies were formed to establish and promote pedigreed breeds. The first cat show as we know them today was held in 1871 at the Crystal Palace in Sydenham, London. The show was staged by Harrison Weir, a cat enthusiast whom many regard as the father of the cat fancy. In all, around 160 cats were present. The show was such a success that exhibiting pedigreed cats suddenly became all the rage among the upper classes in the United Kingdom.

In Britain in 1887, Weir helped form the National Cat Club (NCC), of which he was elected president. The NCC instituted a system of recording the ancestry of purebreds, allowing exhibitors to keep track of their cats' heritage. In 1910, the Governing Council of the Cat Fancy (GCCF) was created to keep the breed registers, to license and control cat shows, to look after the welfare of cats, and to insure that the cat fancy rules were not broken. This association is the main governing body today in the United Kingdom.

The American Cat Fancy

American cat lovers soon caught the cat fancy fever. In the 1870s, cat shows in New England mostly featured the all-American Maine Coon. Soon, however, Persians and Siamese began appearing on the American scene. The first American all-breed cat show was held in 1895 in New York's Madison Square Garden. This show marked the real beginning of the American cat fancy.

When the American cat fancy began, no American cat registries existed. Stud books were kept for a time by a branch of the government. In 1899, however, America's first cat association, the American Cat Association (ACA), formed to keep records of offspring produced by pedigreed cats. Although they are a relatively small association today, they paved the way for the American cat fancy.

Humans learned that felines were invaluable in controlling the rodent populations that destroyed their food supplies, and cats discovered how handy humans were in attracting tasty rodents.

The Cat Fancy Today

Hundreds of cat shows take place in the United States and Canada every year and in almost every other country in the world. Because of the number of cat registries, things are more complicated today than when the cat fancy began. Today, at least ten registries exist in North America: the American Association of Cat Enthusiasts (AACE), the American Cat Association (ACA), the American Cat Fanciers Association (ACFA), the Canadian Cat Association (CCA), the Cat Fanciers Association (CFA), the Cat Fanciers Federation (CFF), the National Cat Fanciers' Association (NCFA), The International Cat Association (TICA), the Traditional Cat Association (TCA), and the United Feline Organization (UFO). Clubs affiliated with the associations, rather than the organizations themselves, generally organize and hold shows. Many differences exist between the associations. Basically, though, they all share the same goals—the improvement and preservation of recognized cat breeds and the promotion and welfare of all domestic cats. They keep stud books and records, maintain breed standards, and register pedigreed cats. They also sanction shows; grant titles and keep track of earned points; provide information and training for breeders, clerks, and judges; communicate with foreign cat associations; feature lectures; issue publications; educate cat owners; and further cat causes. All associations have codes of ethics or policies to help maintain humane standards. Each association has its own set of regulations governing the showing and registering of cats.

One of the associations' most important functions is to keep records. The purpose of registering purebred cats is to give breeders a continuing history of their breed and to ensure that the offspring can be registered and shown.

The Breed Standard

The cat associations keep breed standards on every breed of cat they recognize. These "standards of perfection" are guidelines that describe the characteristics that make a cat a supreme example of its breed. A perfect cat would earn a score of 100 points, but few if any cats can achieve a perfect score. The standard is an ideal for which to strive, not usually an actual description of the breed itself.

The standard is used by the show judges to judge a cat's merit. Therefore, if you plan to show, you need to be familiar with your breed's standard. Since the breed standard can vary, sometimes greatly, from association to association, be sure to obtain a copy of your cat's standard from the association in which you intend to show.

A committee of judges, breeders, and fanciers draft and update the standard as necessary. Keep in mind that the standard is an ideal. A cat that earns no ribbons in the show ring could still make a wonderful companion.

THE FOUR MAJOR BREEDS OF REX

The four most common breeds of Rex Cats are the Cornish Rex, the Devon Rex, the LaPerm, and the Selkirk Rex. Although they are all part of the same family, there are differences between these breeds you should consider.

The Cornish Rex

At first glance, the Cornish Rex might seem like a tiny invader from the planet Rex with its slender-as-a-whip body, huge batlike ears, big eyes, and ultrashort, wavy coat. The Cornish Rex may be extraordinary in appearance, but it is completely catlike in temperament and personality. When combined with its fascinating history, this breed is the most popular of the Rex breeds and was also the first Rex to be accepted by cat fanciers.

History

The first Cornish Rex was born in Cornwall in southwest England, for which the breed is named. Located in one of the warmest and rainiest parts of England, Cornwall was allegedly home to King Arthur's Camelot.

Is this some tiny invasion from the planet Rex? Relax, it's just the rambunctious Cornish, extraordinary in appearance but completely catlike in character.

It is a scenic area of high moors and sandy beaches, hills and low mountains, a place, according to their web site, where "spring arrives early and autumn lingers longer." The poor soil and few resources make tourism the main industry. However, some farms remain, and the people are proud of their Celtic heritage and rich cultural history.

On July 21, 1950, Serena, an ordinary tortoiseshell and white barn cat, gave birth to five kittens on a farm in Bodmin Moor, Cornwall. This now famous litter contained four ordinary kittens and one extraordinary, curly-coated male kitten. Nina Ennismore, Serena's owner, named the kitten Kallibunker. Kallibunker was either cream-colored or red and white, depending on the source of the information. He was very different from his littermates—his hair was short and curly. Instead of possessing the stocky body of his littermates and mother, Kallibunker's body was long and lithe. He had large ears, a slender tail, and an egg-shaped head. This cat was destined to become the father of the Cornish Rex breed.

Intrigued by his unusual appearance, Ennismore kept Kallibunker as a pet. She recognized that Kallibunker's coat was similar to the wavy fur of the Rex rabbit since Ennismore had previously raised and exhibited rabbits. However, not until she talked to British geneticist Mr. A. C. Jude did she begin a breeding program to develop Kallibunker's uniqueness into a recognized breed. The name Cornish Rex was decided upon because of the region in which the breed was found and the breed's resemblance to the Rex rabbit.

Ennismore backcrossed Kallibunker to his mother since his father, a free-roaming straight-haired tom, did not show up to participate in the breeding program. The union of Kallibunker and Serena produced a litter containing one straight-coated kitten and two curly-coated kittens. Only one of these kittens, Poldhu, a curly male, went on to sire kittens.

In 1956 Ennismore stopped breeding. However, by then other breeders had become interested in the Cornish Rex and continued the breeding program. Because of bad luck, fading kitten syndrome caused by blood type incompatibility, inbreeding, and mishaps (according to some sources, Poldhu was rendered sterile by a botched surgical procedure performed to determine his true color), just one fertile Cornish Rex male remained in England by 1960. Only by breeding the remaining male to other breeds such as Burmese and to domestic shorthairs did the British Cornish Rex survive in England.

In 1957, however, two Cornish Rex were brought to America, courtesy of fancier Fran Blancheri of California. One, Pendennis Castle, died shortly after arrival. The other, LaMorna Cove, who arrived pregnant by Poldhu (prior to his untimely encounter with the scalpel), survived and produced a Rex litter that included two curly kittens, Diamond Lil and Marmaduke. These cats became the foundation cats for the Cornish Rex in America.

Since the gene pool was so small and no additional Rex were available from England, the American breeders bred Diamond Lil and Marmaduke together, but all of their kittens died at birth. The Cornish Rex was definitely an endangered species. At that point, outcrossing to other breeds was the only hope. Therefore, they bred Diamond Lil and Marmaduke to Siamese. Soon after, Havana Browns, Russian Blues, American Shorthairs, and British Shorthairs were also added to the bloodline. Not only did this provide the essential genetic diversity, but it also provided the wide selection of colors and patterns available today.

Later, decedents of Laemmchen (the first German Rex, see page 42) and a Rex-coated female named Mystery Lady that was found in a California shelter were used to increase numbers and help the breed attain the genetic diversify it now enjoys. While still an uncommon breed, the Cornish Rex has climbed to the thirteenth most popular breed in the United States and the ninth most popular shorthair, according to the CFA's 1999 registration totals.

Conformation

The Cornish Rex has been compared to the Whippet dog because of its slender athletic build, curved contours, arched back, and willowy body. From torso to tail the Cornish Rex is long and lean. However, do not let the willowy form fool you—the Cornish Rex is no weakling. Under that ultrashort fur are strong bones and muscle as well as teeth and claws for those foolish enough to annoy the self-assured Cornish.

The defining characteristic of the breed, however, is its very short, close-lying, very soft and wavy fur. The entire coat is curly or wavy, sometimes compared to the design of a wash-board. Although completely lacking guard hairs—the long, stiff, outer hairs that act as a barrier against the elements—the Cornish Rex's coat is made up of the soft inner down and awn hairs, with down hair predominating. The lack of guard hairs makes the Cornish Rex's coat very soft to the touch. Fanciers often compare the feel of the Cornish with warm suede or crushed velvet.

Personality

Fans of Cornwall's own breed say that the unique look is only part of the attraction; the personality of the breed is something special. Energetic, intelligent, and people oriented, the Cornish Rex is one of the most active—and interactive—breeds. Fanciers say that a 16-year-old Cornish is just as playful and frisky as a 16-week-old one. The Cornish Rex compares to the Abyssinian and the Bengal in activity level—extremely energetic. Fanciers also note that Cornish Rex have definite senses of humor.

Many Cornish Rex enjoy a good game of fetch and will bring back catnip toys and balls for you to toss again and again. Interactive toys are best; fishing poles with feathers or sparkly streamers and laser light toys are always a hit. Actually, Cornish see everything as toys, and you must put away anything that might be confused with a toy such as rolls of film, cotton swabs, socks—anything movable is fair game to the playful Cornish Rex.

Not only are they active, but they are also nimble climbers, leapers, and sprinters. No cupboard is safe with an agile Cornish Rex in the house. They are very curious (some might say nosy), and they have wonderfully dexterous paws for prying open drawers and twisting doorknobs. They are intelligent, too, and use their considerable powers of observation to figure out ways into forbidden areas.

If you prefer your cats laid back and aloof, the Cornish is not the breed for you. Cornish Rex are not stereotypical aloof and independent cats. They demand attention from their human friends. The Cornish will be on the kitchen counter, tabletop, desk, clothes dryer—wherever you are, the Cornish wants to be.

Cornish Rex are particularly affectionate around dinnertime—so loving, in fact, you cannot keep them out of your plate without a squirt bottle. Dinner will never be dull with a mischievous Cornish Rex stealing food from your plate and then looking at you with big,

CHECKLIST

The Cornish Rex
✔ Origin: Cornwall, England
✔ Date of Birth: 1950
✔ Hair Length: very short
✔ Weight: adult males 6 to 9 pounds (2.7 to 4.1 kg); adult females 5 to 7 pounds (2.3 to 3.2 kg)
✔ Colors and Patterns: all colors and patterns accepted, including the Siamese pointed pattern
✔ Status: accepted for championship by all cat associations

Cornish Rex come in virtually all possible colors and patterns.

Buying Tips

Cornish Rex breeders are fairly rare. Therefore Cornish Rex kittens and cats can be hard to come by, particularly if you have a specific color, gender, or age in mind. Seeing the cattery, the kittens, and the parents before agreeing to buy is always best. However, it is not always possible when you are looking for a Cornish.

Some breeders will ship kittens if you can't find a breeder in your area. If you must buy a kitten sight unseen, ask for pictures and references. Also check out the breeder with the breeder's cat association.

Pet- and breeder-quality Cornish Rex kittens sell for $350 to $700. Some breeders, though, do not sell breeder-quality kittens, reasoning that if a cat is not good enough to show, it should not be bred. Show-quality kittens cost $1,000 and up, sometimes *well* up for kittens with excellent bloodlines and show prospects.

Of course, the price depends upon geographic location, bloodline, and breeder as well as pattern and coat color. Breeders note that pedigree cats are more expensive in metropolitan areas.

Since the breed is relatively rare, breeders often have waiting lists. You will probably have to wait at least a few months to get your Cornish Rex. Breeders generally release their kittens

innocent eyes as if to say, "Who, me?" They love to eat. Efforts must be made to keep them from becoming decidedly pear shaped in their later years (see page 67).

When not paid the proper amount of attention, Cornish make their feelings known. While not as vocal as Siamese, they do let you know when all is not right in their cat-dom. Fortunately, their voices are not as penetrating as Siamese.

Cornish Rex. Notice the rippling waves that characterize the Cornish's coat.

Even the whiskers of the Cornish Rex are curly.

around 16 weeks of age to ensure the kittens have had all their inoculations and the important weeks of quality time with Mom and siblings.

Sometimes, adult Cornish Rex retired from breeding programs or from show careers are placed with good homes, and this is a good way to get a show-quality Rex less expensively. These cats can make wonderful pets, and you don't have to deal with the mischief a young Rex kitten can make. Retired Cornish run between $50 and $300, although the price varies according to location, breeder, and cat.

Common colors and patterns include solid white, blue, black, bicolor, black smoke, and red tabby, although virtually every color and pattern is recognized. However, since the breed is comparatively rare, not all colors are available. If you are looking for a pet, be flexible about color and gender, and you will have an easier time acquiring a Cornish. Remember beauty is only fur deep; the important thing is to acquire a Cornish Rex that will be a great companion.

The Devon Rex

The Devon Rex, with its satellite dish ears, large alert eyes, long, thin body, and short, wavy fur, provokes exclamations from folks new to this unique breed. Its short, curly coat and the fact that the Devon wags its tail when happy have led to its nickname "the Poodle cat."

History

The breed can be traced back to a single cat. In 1960, a woman named Beryl Cox of Buck-

fastleigh, Devon, England, noticed a curly-haired feral tomcat living in the deserted tin mine near her home. In due time, this curly-haired transient fathered the kittens of a straight-coated calico female who was also hanging around. She delivered her now legendary litter in Cox's garden. One of the kittens took after his father—he had the same short, curly coat.

Cox, quite taken with the kitten that looked like a little pixie with his huge ears and mole-gray curls, decided to take him away from his uncertain life as a feral feline. She adopted him and named him, appropriately enough, Kirlee. Aware of the Cornish Rex that had been discovered ten years earlier, Cox thought that Kirlee might be a member of that breed. She contacted Brian Sterling-Webb, a breeder who was working with the Cornish, and he was excited to hear about Cox's find.

CHECKLIST

The Devon Rex

✔ Origin: Buckfastleigh, Devon, England
✔ Date of Birth: 1960
✔ Hair Length: very short
✔ Weight: adult males 8 to 10 pounds (3.6 to 4.5 kg); adult females 5 to 8 pounds (2.3 to 3.6 kg)
✔ Colors and Patterns: all colors and patterns accepted, including the Siamese pointed pattern
✔ Status: accepted for championship by all cat associations

However, it soon became apparent that Kirlee was not a Cornish Rex since matings between Kirlee and Cornish queens produced nothing but straight-coated kittens. The gene governing Kirlee's coat was soon discovered to be recessive. Fanciers now believe that Kirlee's parents must have been related since a recessive gene must be present in both parents to affect the physical appearance of the offspring.

At this point, Cox knew she had a brand new breed. A breeding program was set up, and Kirlee was introduced to several British Shorthair beaus. All the resulting kittens were straight-coated (both parents must have the Rex gene, remember). When his daughters were bred back to Kirlee, though, the litters contained 50 percent curly-haired kittens. All Devon Rex can trace their lineage back to Kirlee.

At first, a few problems arose. A seemingly hairless gene in the Devon's makeup produced cats with bare patches on their necks and undersides. Some did not have any hair at all, and breeders were concerned about the appeal of bald cats. Strangely enough, however, this didn't seem to affect their popularity with the cat-loving public. Devon owners knitted little jackets for their unclad kitties, and their Devons did not seem to mind getting dressed up before going outside to play. Fortunately, breeders worked to eliminate this problem in subsequent litters, and today baldness is increasingly rare.

In 1967, the Governing Council of the Cat Fancy (GCCF) recognized that the Cornish Rex and the Devon Rex were two separate breeds and allowed them to compete independently. This was an important step for the Devon. The Devon fanciers knew that the Cornish and the Devon were separate breeds, but the cat associations took some convincing.

The first invasion of North America from the planet Rex happened the very next year, 1968, masterminded by Marion White of Austin, Texas. In 1979, the Devon Rex Breed Club formed to organize Devon lovers and to promote the breed with the U.S. cat associations.

Four years later, in 1972, the ACFA became the first U.S. association to recognize the Devon Rex. The CFA turned out to be the most difficult association to convince of the Devon's originality. For a number of years, fanciers struggled to persuade the CFA to separate the Devon from the Cornish. In 1983, the CFA finally recognized the Devon for championship in its own right.

By then, U.S. fanciers were working hard to establish the breed, expand the gene pool, and keep up with the demand for pet Devon Rex. Because the breed began with a single cat, Devons were outcrossed with other breeds to widen the gene pool and keep the cats healthy. The practice continues today since the gene pool remains relatively small.

Over the years, the Devon Rex breed has been crossed with British Shorthairs, American Shorthairs, and, during the foundation of the breed, Burmese. Since the purpose of such crosses is to provide new bloodlines while keeping the traits for which the Devon Rex is celebrated, breeders carefully choose the partners for their Devon parents-to-be. They try to choose American and British Shorthairs that are not necessarily outstanding examples of their breeds but, rather, have desirable Devon characteristics. In the CFA, outcrosses to American and British Shorthairs will be allowed until May 1, 2003. Even though some still consider the Devon a minority breed, its popularity in the showrings is growing. The Devon is just behind the Cornish Rex in popularity—fourteenth most popular breed in the United States and the tenth most popular shorthair, according to the CFA's 1999 registration totals.

Conformation

People who attend cat shows who have never seen Devons often ask if they have been shaved, trimmed, or given perms. Devons are just born that way—with exquisitely soft, fine, full-bodied wash-and-wear hair. The coat whirls in every direction or curls tightly in rows.

Unlike the Cornish's coat, the Devon's coat contains all three hair types (guard, awn, and down). However, the guard hairs are typically fragile and stunted, and the whisker hairs are often missing altogether. The hairs break easily. Therefore this breed can develop bald patches that remain until the next hair growth cycle, typically in fall and spring. Too, Devons may go through periods of molting when they are young, usually around eight weeks, six months, and ten months. Hormonal and other events can disrupt that schedule, however, and not all Devons experience molts. During molting, the coat thins out and bald spots may appear. Bare or bald patches are serious faults in the show Devon.

Because the Devon's hair is so short, sparse, and fine, shedding is minimal. One of the major advantages of owning a Devon is that you will spend less time vacuuming, dusting, and grooming your cat (see page 77).

Devons have been compared to pixies, elves and, of course, space aliens for their jumbo-sized satellite dish ears, and large, mischievous, window-to-the-soul eyes. The ideal Devon is medium in size and, despite the slender body style, is solid, muscular, and feels surprisingly heavy when hefted. The Devon's head is a modified wedge, delineated by a narrowing series of three convex curves: the outer edge of the ears, cheekbones, and whisker pads. The muzzle is short, the chin strong, and the face is full cheeked with pronounced cheekbones and whisker break.

The characteristic ears are set very low on the head and are very wide at the base so that the outside base of the ear extends beyond the line of the wedge. The large, oval eyes slope toward the outer edges of the ears, adding to the elfin look.

Because of the diversity of their predecessors, Devons come in an amazing variety of colors and pattern combinations.

Personality

This breed has a personality all its own, according to owners of the playful Poodle puss. That's one of the reasons for the breed's rise in popularity among cat lovers. If you are looking for the proverbial aloof, independent cat, do not buy a Devon Rex.

Devons are playful, curious, and active, but not as active as the Cornish. Devons want to be with you every moment of every day, participating in your every activity, huge ears cocked in curiosity, large eyes glistening with affection, agile paws reaching to tap you if you are not giving them your full attention. For active, inquisitive cats, however, Devons are even-tempered and adaptable to most situations.

In a household of these charmers, you'll find that the Devons stick together but will readily cuddle with other breeds if no other Devons are present. Their favorite playmates, however, are people. By being extraordinarily social, Devons will do just about anything to get your attention. They excel at playing fetch and enjoy any game that requires your active participation.

Devons are also known for their insatiable appetites. After all, they need a lot of energy to race around the house without touching the floor. Unless you want a Devon

While both the Cornish and the Devon Rex have large ears and eyes, the head shape and ear placement are very different.

clinging to your leg like a huge curly-haired tick, you better be on time with the cat food. They like human food, too—they come right up on the table and steal food off your plate, your fork, and sometimes right out of your mouth. They also have peculiar appetites; seeing a Devon munching on pasta, cantaloupe, or avocado is not uncommon. Some even eat bananas.

Devons are not overly vocal, which is a definite plus. If they spoke their minds, they might be a bit too obtrusive. That is not to say they do not communicate when they

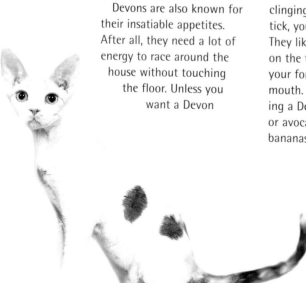

The Devon Rex's unique short, wavy coat is velvety soft to the touch.

Devons enjoy each other's company, but will readily cuddle with other breeds if no other Devons are available.

have something to say. They chirp and twitter rather than meow. Some are even adept at the silent meow, where their mouths open but nothing comes out.

The Devon has all three hair types but the guard hairs are typically fragile and stunted, and the whisker hairs are often missing altogether.

Devons will keep you laughing with their antics. As highly intelligent and keen observers of human nature, Devons are known for their talent for getting into adorable mischief. Just try keeping them off the counter—Devons can be tenacious in their curiosity. Because of their curiosity and ability to fly through the air with the greatest of ease, no shelf or cupboard is safe from the inquiring mind of the Devon. They are not averse to people climbing, either, and enjoy perching on available shoulders.

Buying Tips

Breeders recommend that you begin your search for the perfect Devon at least six months in advance or even a bit longer, because Devon demand exceeds supply. Reputable breeders usually have their kittens sold soon after they are born and almost always have waiting lists.

No Devon should leave home before it is at least 14 weeks old—beware of breeders who would let them go earlier, before the kittens have had the important socialization time with their mothers. Buy from a breeder who really seems to care about matching you with the kitten you want. A good breeder wants the purchaser and the kitten to be happy. Commonly, breeders either alter pet-quality kittens before they go to their new homes or withhold the kitten's papers until proof of alteration is provided.

As for the price of the perfect Devon, expect to spend between $400 and $500 for pet quality. For a breeder-quality Devon, you will pay around $600 to $850, depending upon the quality and the bloodline. Show quality will set you back $600 to $1,500. Breeder- and show-quality cats are usually sold only to established

fanciers. Unless you will be showing your Devon, you will want pet quality anyway.

The LaPerm

When you first glimpse the original new wave cat of Oregon, you might think you were seeing a cat just back from the hairdresser, but only Mother Nature has styled this breed's curly locks. Also called the Dalles LaPerm, the LaPerm is a relatively new Rex and currently quite rare. However, the breed has fanciers talking. Although not yet widely recognized by the cat associations, the LaPerm is nevertheless steadily gaining fanciers because an appealing personality comes with the curly hairdo.

History

The story of the LaPerm's origins is the same as the rest of the Rex breeds—it arose spontaneously from the domestic cat gene pool. In 1980, Linda and Richard Koehl, seeking a quieter life than the Los Angeles area provided, bought a 10-acre (4 ha) cherry orchard in The Dalles, Oregon. Since the rich agricultural valley was replete with rodents, they bought two cats to control the mice inhabiting the farm's barns. This feline pair spent pleasant days romping around the cherry trees and ridding the barns of mice. Like most barn cats, they came and went as they pleased. Since unaltered cats happily reproduce themselves, nature soon took its course. In summer 1982, Speedy, the Koehl's gray tabby, speedily gave birth to a litter of six.

One of the kittens, however, looked very different from her littermates. Instead of the fine down that covered the bodies of her siblings, she was completely bald. She weighed less than her littermates but had a longer body and larger ears. Linda Koehl thought she was the ugliest kitten she had ever seen and figured the kitten would die.

The kitten did not, however. At about eight weeks, soft, curly hair began sprouting from the kitten's body. Koehl named the kitten Curly. Although not a breeder at the time nor even really a cat person, Koehl had no idea that what she had was unusual.

As Curly grew, Koehl realized that Curly not only had a unique coat but had such a charming temperament that Koehl found herself becoming a bonafide cat lover. Not only was her short, curly hair soft and inviting to touch, but Curly's affection was gentle and trusting. She was very loving but not in a pushy, demanding way.

Curly soon produced her own litter of five male brown tabby kittens, all of which were bald at birth. These five, like their mother, soon grew crops of curly hair. As soon as they were old enough, the five toms enthusiastically set about to pass on their unique coats. One of the males hiked across the street to mate with a neighbor's black shorthaired female. The result was five curly kittens, all of which the Koehls recovered and added to their rapidly increasing group of curly cats.

Over the next five years, the Koehls made no effort to breed Curly and her offspring selectively—they just let nature take its course. Sadly, Curly disappeared one night, never to return. However, her legacy continued at the rate of two to eight per litter until the Koehl farm was as overrun with curly cats as it had once been with rodents.

Finally, Linda Koehl sought to learn more about the unusual cats. She discovered that both males and females were capable of passing on the curly coat. She also found that only one parent needed to have the curly coat to pass along the trait. Anyone with a bit of knowledge about genetics will tell you that means the coat was governed by a dominant gene.

Finally, Koehl rounded up all her curly cats and began to control the breeding. She named the breed LaPerm, which implied *wavy* in several languages. After doing some more reading about cat breeds, Koehl decided to introduce her cats to the cat fancy. In 1992, she took four LaPerms to a CFA show in Portland, unprepared for the interest and excitement the cats would generate. Her cage of curly cats was soon surrounded by a crowd of curious and captivated cat fanciers.

Inspired by the enthusiasm of the cat people at that first show, Koehl attended shows on a

CHECKLIST

The LaPerm
✔ Origin: The Dalles, Oregon, United States
✔ Date of Birth: 1982
✔ Hair Length: shorthaired and longhaired varieties
✔ Weight: adult males 7 to 9 pounds (3.2 to 4.1 kg); adult females 5 to 7 pounds (2.3 to 3.2 kg)
✔ Colors and Patterns: all colors and patterns accepted, including the Siamese pointed pattern
✔ Status: recognized by TICA and UFO in the new breed and color (NBC) class and in the CFA in the miscellaneous class

Longhaired female LaPerm. The hair is medium long and the curls range from tight ringlets to long corkscrew curls.

regular basis. With the help of geneticists and other breeders who joined the crusade, she established her Kloshe Cattery, began an organized breeding program, and started the long and involved process of gaining recognition from the cat associations.

At the time of this writing, the LaPerm is recognized by TICA and the UFO as a new

LaPerms may differ in their color and coats, but most share the great personality characteristic to the breed.

Chocolate lynx point LaPerm shorthair. The coat is soft and wavy over the shoulders, back, and undersides.

breed and color (NBC) and in the CFA in the miscellaneous class. This means the breed has been accepted for registration by these associations and can be shown but is not yet accepted for championship competition. LaPerms can earn awards in the NBC class but not in the miscellaneous class, and they cannot compete in the championship class until the breed is accepted for championship. LaPerm fanciers are working to meet the requirements for championship competition.

Conformation

The characteristic curly coat comes in both longhaired and shorthaired varieties. In the shorthaired LaPerm, the coat is soft and wavy over the shoulders, back, and undersides. In the longhaired variety, the hair is medium long and the curls range from tight ringlets to long corkscrew curls, resembling the hair style

Longhaired LaPerms. At birth, LaPerm kittens can be bald, curly, or straight-haired. The coat develops as the cat matures.

called the "shag." Combine that with a long, semiforeign body, ears with fancy lynx tippings, a broad wedge-shaped head, and expressive, almond-shaped eyes, and you have the unique look of the LaPerm.

LaPerm kittens can be born bald, with curly hair or with straight hair. The coat changes so much as the kittens grow that telling what any kitten will look like as an adult is virtually impossible. Some of the straight-haired kittens grow up to become regular straight-haired cats, but some sprout curls as they mature. The first six months of life are a guessing game. Too, most LaPerms go through an ugly-duckling period before their first birthday in which they lose almost all of their fur. In short order, however, they turn back into swans as the fur grows back curlier and thicker than before.

Like all cats, LaPerms shed. According to fanciers, though, they do not shed as much as cats with normal hair. However, some LaPerms will go through several molting periods in their lives, where they lose much of their hair. LaPerms molt during periods of hormonal activity such as puberty and pregnancy. While every LaPerm will go through at least one stage of dropping part or all of its coat during its lifetime, altering will generally stop repeated molting since it eliminates the hormonal changes that trigger the molt.

Personality

Regardless of the length and curliness of the fur, one thing stays the same—the great personality of these cats. So important is personality to this breed that the ideal temperament is mentioned in the TICA breed standard: "Inquisitive by nature and always wanting to know what is going on around them, kittens have been known to quit nursing and seek out the source of a human voice even before their eyes are open."

LaPerms are gentle, affectionate, and blossom with human companionship, achieving their best personality with consistent human interaction. While always present when their human friends are around, they want to be involved in whatever you are doing. While extremely people oriented, they are very curious and inquisitive as well. They are not overly vocal, but LaPerms will nevertheless tell you when something is terribly amiss, like empty food dishes. They do enjoy an occasional conversation with their favorite humans, however. Unlike some breeds, many LaPerms enjoy being held, either in your arms or drooped over a shoulder. Breeders note that LaPerms adapt well to apartment living because of their strong bond with their human companions.

Buying Tips

You can expect to pay from $250 to $450 for a pet-quality LaPerm. This price may include the cost of spaying and neutering since some breeders do this before releasing pet-quality cats. Some breeders advise purchasing a kitten after the surgery has been performed since the kittens seem to adjust to their new homes better after alteration. Too, the surgery is less stressful if performed while the cats are in a familiar environment.

For a breeder-quality LaPerm, expect to pay around $800, the recommended price of the LaPerm Society of America. Show quality may be more, depending upon the breeder and area. If you are looking to show your LaPerm, keep in mind that not all associations recognize this new breed. Because this breed is new and still being developed, the breed has an open registry, which means LaPerms can be bred with ordinary straight-haired domestic cats. The gene pool will remain open until a sufficiently large gene pool has been established. This is a wise policy—some new breeds have been virtually ruined when breeders closed the gene pool too soon in the breed's evolution. So while the breed does have a breed standard with a specific conformation, considerable variation can be seen from cat to cat and from breeder to breeder. Because of this diversity, the LaPerm comes in all colors and patterns, including the Siamese pointed pattern. The hair length and fullness vary, too, depending upon the bloodline, season, and maturity of the cat. When choosing a kitten, look for curly whiskers, because this means the coat will also be curly.

Be sure the LaPerm kittens you are considering buying are registered with at least one of the cat associations that recognize the LaPerm. Papers are particularly important if you plan to breed or show. Without papers, you cannot be sure that you have a genuine LaPerm, and you might be required to compete in the household pet category should you choose to show.

The Selkirk Rex

Curly, exquisitely plush, with a coat that cascades in colorful spirals, the Selkirk Rex is perfect if you like the permed look. While often described as a cat in sheep's clothing, the Selkirk is the newest of the recognized Rex breeds. The first Selkirk was discovered in 1987, which makes it a rookie Rex compared with the Devon and Cornish. Even the LaPerm has been catting around for five years longer than the Selkirk.

Being the new Rex on the block has not stopped the Selkirk from gaining quick recognition from the cat associations, however, and admiration from cat lovers all across the country. Since its discovery in 1987, the Selkirk has achieved acceptance in ACA, ACFA, CCA, CFA, TICA, and UFO. This is quite an accomplishment for a breed that, if not for serendipity, would have taken that final walk down a shelter's death row.

History

The first Selkirk was discovered by shelter worker Peggy Vorrhees of the Bozeman Humane Society animal shelter in Wyoming in 1987. The kitten, a dilute calico female, had an unusual coat that resembled lamb's wool. However, she had come from an entirely ordinary batch of domestic cats produced by an ordinary queen with straight hair.

CHECKLIST

The Selkirk Rex
✔ Origin: Wyoming, United States
✔ Date of Birth: 1987
✔ Hair Length: shorthaired and longhaired varieties
✔ Weight: adult males 8 to 12 pounds (3.6 to 5.4 kg); adult females 7 to 10 pounds (3.2 to 4.5 kg)
✔ Colors and Patterns: all colors and patterns accepted, including the Siamese pointed pattern
✔ Status: accepted for championship in ACA, TICA, and UFO, provisional status in CFA, new breed and color in ACFA and CCA

Vorrhees, who had purchased a Persian from longtime breeder Jeri Newman, took the kitten to Newman in Livingston, Montana. Newman, fascinated by cats in general and cat genetics in particular, had made it known that she was interested in any cats that were in any way unusual. The kitten—cute, curious, and curly—was certainly that. As plush and huggable as a child's stuffed toy with curly whiskers, ears full of curly ear furnishings, fur that looked like it had received a body wave, the kitten was just what Newman was looking for.

Newman soon found that not only did the kitten have a unique coat, she had an appealing personality, too. She named the kitten Miss DePesto of Noface (Noface is the cattery name) because she followed Newman everywhere, pestering her for love and attention. When Pest came of age, Newman bred her to Photo Finish of Deekay, one of her black Persian males. The mating produced a litter of six—three of which had the distinctive curly coat. Since Newman had curled up with many a book on genetics, she knew that this meant the gene governing the curly coat was dominant. Only one parent need possess the gene for the trait to appear in the offspring, and the ratio of straight to curly coats would be approximately 50 percent if the other parent did not possess the gene.

A dominant gene is a boon to breeders since a curly-coated cat can be bred to a straight-coated cat and still produce some curly kittens. The only disadvantage is that about 50 percent of those kittens are born with straight coats and do not carry the Rex gene at all. Therefore, the straight-coated cannot be used in a breeding program.

Newman experimented with a few more test litters, including mating Pest back to her son, a curly black and white shorthair named Noface Oscar Kowalski. This litter produced three more curly kittens,

Selkirks are well-known for their cuddliness, and they make affectionate companions.

including one longhair. Therefore, not only did Pest carry the dominant curl gene but also the recessive longhair gene since both Oscar and Pest had to possess the longhair gene to produce a longhaired offspring.

Oscar and Pest produced another litter, this time producing a curly red point male that Newman named Noface Snowman of Manawyddan. This proved that Pest also carried the recessive gene for the Siamese colorpoint pattern, which she had passed to her son.

It became clear to Newman that the curly coat was unique in the cat fancy and should be developed into a recognized breed. Because

This longhaired tortoiseshell Selkirk Rex female has a lovely facial pattern.

Shorthaired cream Selkirk Rex.

of this interesting variety of genes and colors, Newman decided that all colors and both hair lengths would be allowed from the start. She wrote a breed standard and, since Pest's body type was rather unbalanced and gawky, she wrote the standard to describe the more balanced look of the British Shorthair. With his rounded, half-Persian body style, Oscar was much closer to the ideal than his mother and was the father of most of the Selkirk lines existing today. She decided on the name Selkirk Rex for her new breed because her stepfather's family name was Selkirk.

Newman went on to combine the qualities of the Exotic, British Shorthair, and American Shorthair into her Selkirk bloodlines. New-

Longhaired tortie point Selkirk Rex kitten. Selkirks have easy-going personalities, but they do enjoy playtime, too.

man approached breeders who were working with breeds she was interested in adding to her Selkirk lines. She asked if they would be interested in working with the new breed. Some accepted the challenge and helped to further the Selkirk's cause. Jeri Newman has since gone on to other things.

Only three years after the breed's discovery, the Selkirk was presented to TICA's board of directors and was accepted into the new breed and color class. In February 1992, the CFA accepted the breed for registration in the miscellaneous class. At the time of this writing, the Selkirk is accepted for championship in ACA, TICA, and UFO, provisional status in CFA, and NBC in ACFA and CCA. Fanciers credit the Selkirk's unusual look and the breeders' concerted efforts for the Selkirk's quick acceptance.

Conformation

Because of the outcrossings used, the Selkirk possesses a *cobby* body style—stocky, muscular, substantially boned, with a rectangular, muscular torso. The ideal Selkirk's head is round and full cheeked, with a short, squared-off muzzle that creates an excellent showcase for the curly whiskers—yes, they curl, too. The full cheeks and large, round eyes contribute to the breed's characteristic sweet expression. The ears are medium sized, pointed, and set well apart on the gently rounded head. Of the four Rex breeds, the Selkirk is the only one with a cobby body type.

As for the unique coat, all three hair types (guard, awn, and down) are curly, with the curl more pronounced around the neck and tail. The guard hairs are slightly coarse, but the overall effect is a soft and plush coat. The hair has a soft, flowing, elegant feel, and the texture is very light. The curl goes all the way down to the skin.

Considerable difference exists between the longhaired and shorthaired varieties of the breed. The coat of the shorthaired Selkirk is plush, medium in length, and curls over the entire body. In the longhair, the dense, semi-long coat hangs in loose, individual ringlets and has a more dramatic look. The curls are particularly prominent around the neck and on the tail. In both hair lengths, the fur is soft and dense. All colors and patterns of the cat spectrum are accepted.

The coat goes through several stages as the cat develops. Selkirk kittens are curly at birth, then around four months of age suddenly lose their curls. The curls come back again beginning at about eight months. The coat becomes curlier every month until the cats are about two years old. The amount of curl varies from cat to cat. Climate and both seasonal and hormonal changes can also influence the coat's curliness. A humid climate increases the curliness of the fur, just as it will human tresses.

Homozygous Selkirks (cats that have two copies of the Rex gene) are highly prized by breeders. These cats can be bred with an outcrossing that does not possess the Rex gene, and all the resulting kittens will have the curly coat. Cats with two copies of the gene have curlier, tighter, and sparser fur than cats that possess only one copy of the gene. Unfortunately, homozygous Selkirks are few and far between.

Since the gene pool is still quite small and the negative effects of inbreeding a real concern, Selkirks can be bred to a select handful of other breeds that share the cobby conformation of the Selkirk.

Personality

Not only are Selkirks cute and cuddly, but they make affectionate companions as well. Selkirks are gentle, sweet, playful cats that love to be loved. By being very people oriented and not shy about sharing their affection, Selkirks make good family pets.

Selkirks are known for their mellow personalities and laid-back temperaments. They take life as it comes and tend to be easygoing, tolerant, and patient—courtesy of the British Shorthair, Exotic, and Persian influences. However, they are not couch potatoes; the American Shorthair and Exotic influences ensure a playful, fun-loving personality. They enjoy a good game of fetch and particularly enjoy games in which their owners take an active role.

As ever-present companions, Selkirks enjoy being held and cuddled, often seeking out their favorite human's lap. Some even want to ride on their owners' shoulders to get a bird's-eye view of the action. They are not as vocal as some breeds, but they will let you know if all is not right in their world.

Even though they are mellow and easygoing, they are curious and clever. Owners report that Selkirks can learn tricks you would rather they did not, like opening doors and cupboards. Fortunately, they are easy to train (for cats) and will listen to reason if you use the proper training methods.

Buying Tips

At the time of this writing, Selkirks are expensive and hard to come by. Since they are so rare (only 121 were registered with the CFA in 1999) and since breeders are working to satisfy the requirements of CFA championship status, most Selkirks that possess the Rex gene are kept for breeding. Breeding females are particularly in demand. It's very difficult, if not impossible, for a novice cat fancier to obtain one at any price. Breeding stock is generally placed with British Shorthair, Exotic, and Persian breeders who are also interested in breeding Selkirks. The waiting list can be long. The average wait for a Selkirk is between six months and a year, and sometimes longer, particularly if you are looking for pet quality. However, straight-coated Selkirks can be obtained quite quickly and easily, and considerably more cheaply, than curly Selkirks. These cats lack the Rex gene and so do not possess the trademark curly coat. Therefore, they are not useful for breeding programs. They do, however, possess the Selkirk body style and personality. If a curly coat is not important to you, you might consider a straight-coated Selkirk. Price varies; consult a breeder in your area for pricing information.

Since the cat fancy began in the late 1800s, the art of cat breeding and creating new breeds has become something of a national pastime. More than half of the breeds currently recognized by cat associations have existed for less than 50 years.

New Rex Breeds

The Rex mutation has occurred spontaneously in domestic cats many times over the last 60 years and in many different parts of the world. Some of these varieties have since died out because no effort was made to preserve them. Others contributed to the advancement of other Rex breeds. Some others still exist, though not in large numbers. A few of these are briefly covered here, but this list is certainly not exhaustive. While these breeds are not as well known as the four covered in this book, nevertheless they are relevant to the history of Rex breeds.

New Rex breeds will likely appear in the future, either by spontaneous mutation or by crosses between existing breeds. Since the Rex mutation occurs readily and since Rex breeds are attractive and appealing, some of these new breeds will most likely be accepted by the cat associations in the future if fanciers properly promote and breed them. New cat breeds are classified as either spontaneous mutations (like the Cornish, Devon, Selkirk, and LaPerm) or as hybrids. These are created by breeding together two or more previously known breeds to create a breed with qualities of both (like the Skookum, see page 43).

Keep in mind, however, that anyone can cross two existing breeds and give the offspring a new name. That does not make it a new breed. Years of painstaking work are needed to get a new variety recognized. The requirements for acceptance of new breeds are stringent and vary depending upon the cat association. Even when the requirements are met, no guarantee is made that the breed will be accepted. Acceptance is usually decided by a committee or the board of the association. Sometimes a new breed is opposed by cat fanciers if it possesses some trait of which fanciers disapprove.

German Rex

The German Rex predates the Cornish Rex, the oldest of our recognized Rex breeds, by a few years. Dr. Rose Scheuer-Karpin discovered the first German Rex, a curly-haired black female, among the feral cats on the former grounds of Hufeland Hospital in Berlin, Germany in August of 1951. However, the cat had been a resident of the hospital since around 1947, according to Scheuer-Karpin's account of the events. Scheuer-Karpin described the cat's coat as short and wavy with a fine, silken texture.

Scheuer-Karpin adopted the cat and named her Laemmchen. Matings to her black house-mate, Blackie, produced unexceptional straight-haired black kittens. However, when Laemmchen was mated with one of her sons, Friedolin, in 1957, three of the four resulting black kittens had wavy hair like their mother, indicating that the gene governing the coat mutation was recessive. The Berlin Cat Club showed little interest in Scheuer-Karpin's curly cats. Not until she sent some of her cats to Professor Etienne Letard in Paris, France did the breed begin to receive some attention. Professor Letard began a systematic breeding program using Laemmchen's offspring. While Scheuer-Karpin did not establish a formal breeding program, she encouraged Laemmchen to mate with cats possessing the recessive Rex gene—namely, her sons. Until her death in 1964, Laemmchen produced two litters a year. By the time of her death, she had mothered a verifiable army of curly-coated German Rex and straight-coated cats possessing the reces-sive Rex gene. Fanciers continued to work with the breed. Although rare, the German Rex is now recognized as a breed in its own right in a handful of countries including Germany and Australia.

A number of Laemmchen's offspring were imported to America. Test matings with Cor-nish Rex showed the German Rex and the Cor-nish Rex to carry the same coat mutation because German Rex/Cornish Rex crosses result in curly kittens, which does not occur when incompatible Rex varieties are bred together. The German Rex has a heavier bone structure, rounder head, smaller ears, and a less svelte body type than the Cornish, and the coat is thicker and more uniform as well. However, like the Cornish, the German Rex completely lacks guard hairs.

In the late 1960s and early 1970s, Laemm-chen's offspring were used to expand the Cor-nish Rex gene pool in America since numbers of Cornish Rex were small at that time and breeding stock limited. While the German Rex has yet to be recognized as a breed in the Unites States, it played an important role in the development of the Cornish Rex.

Oregon Rex

The Oregon Rex was discovered in Oregon in 1959. Not much is known about the variety other than it had an American Shorthair body style and a Rex coat. The Oregon variety has thicker awn hairs than the other breeds. Test matings done between the Oregon and the Cornish proved that the Oregon Rex mutation is governed by a recessive gene unlike that of the Cornish Rex, because all offspring were straight-coated. Apparently, little effort has been made to promote the Oregon Rex as a breed in its own right, or efforts to promote it failed, and it may no longer exist.

Ural Rex

Reportedly, this Rex breed has existed in the middle Urals region since World War II. The Ural Rex has a wavy coat that comes in two lengths—short and semilong. The coat is dense and well curled; the whiskers are wavy. The semilonghaired version is not popular because of the "sloppy" quality to the coat.

As a medium-sized cat, the Ural has a strong, muscular body, triangular-shaped head, rounded muzzle, a long, strong neck, medium-sized ears, and rounded, slightly bulging eyes. It has been determined that the gene governing the Ural is different from the Cornish gene, but no testing has been done with the Devon.

Skookum

The Skookum was created in 1996 by a mating between a male Munchkin and a female LaPerm, producing a litter of four Munchkin/LaPerm hybrids. All four kittens had Daddy's short legs and Mommy's curly coat. The natural mutation responsible for the Munchkin's short legs is a dominant genetic trait, as is the LaPerm's curly hair. That means only one parent need have each gene to pass it to offspring.

TICA and UFO encouraged the owners of the cats, Roy and Lynn Galusha of Washington State, to promote the cats as a new breed rather than as a new coat variety of the Munchkin. They chose the name Skookum, a Chinook American Indian word meaning mighty, powerful, or great. At the time of this writing, at least four breeders have joined the Galushas in breeding and promoting the Skookum, which is currently recognized in the provisional class by the UFO.

Bohemia Rex

Some difference of opinion exists as to whether this is a hybrid or a natural mutation. While also called the Czech Curly Cat, the Tsjechian Curly Cat, and the curly Persian, this breed has long, curly hair. According to reports, the Bohemia Rex possesses the same Rex gene as the Cornish Rex. Its origins can supposedly be traced back to a curly kitten born in 1981 to two straight-haired Persians named Adonis and Apoline who lived in the province of Podjestedi in the town of Libereçç in the Czech Republic. Other reports say the breed originated from a deliberate cross between a Persian and a Cornish Rex in an effort to produce a curly-coated Persian. It has not been accepted by the Federation Internationale Feline (FIFe) because of its alleged unmanageable coat and poor body type.

Poodle Cat

This breed, created in Germany around 1992, is a deliberate cross between Scottish Folds, Devon Rex, and European Shorthairs. The idea was to create a cat with the body style and curly hair of the Devon and the folded ears of the Scottish Fold.

According to sources, the breed's originator plans to introduce Manx into the mix to create a curly-haired cat with folded ears and no tail. Its current status is not known. According to accounts, though, it may soon be outlawed because German law prohibits breeding detrimental mutations. The genes that govern both the Scottish Fold and the Manx are known to cause health problems, and so such a breeding program is likely to come to grief.

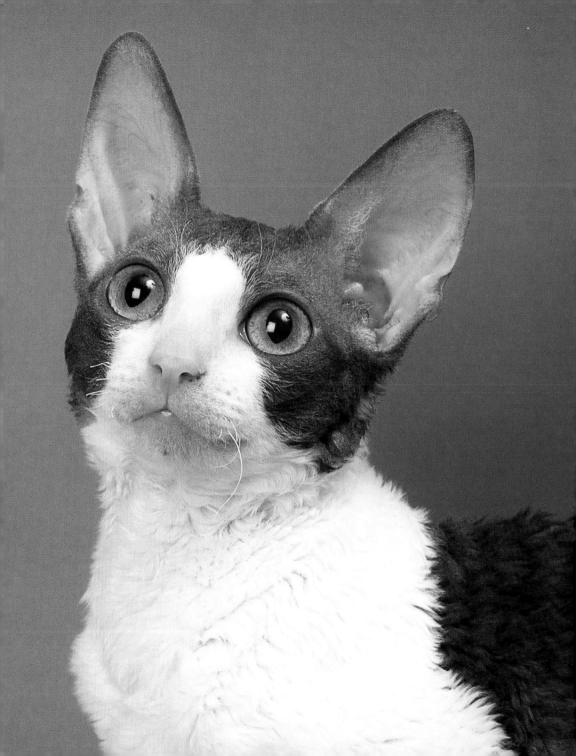

ACQUIRING YOUR REX

As with all important decisions, buying a Rex requires careful consideration. Remember, you are about to embark upon a relationship that may span 15 years or more. Many marriages don't last that long. Spend some time finding the right Rex for you.

Before You Buy

Rex are generally affectionate cats that need attention and quality playtime to be happy. This requires a time commitment on your part. While any breed of cat will require care, Rex cats, with their people-oriented personalities, tend to need more attention than some breeds.

If you work all day and have an active social life at night, take this into consideration before getting any kind of cat. A bored, lonely cat is less destructive than a bored, lonely dog, but a cat will still find ways of expressing her displeasure. To experience fully the rich relationship you can have with Callie, you need to spend your most precious resource with her—time.

Questions to Ask Yourself

Before committing to buy a Rex or any cat, ask yourself these questions:

✔ Are you able and willing to devote a portion of each day to feeding, grooming, and playing with your Rex?

Bicolor Cornish Rex.

✔ Are you financially able to provide for her comfort and health, including the expense of quality cat food, visits to the veterinarian, medications, toys, and quality supervision when you go on vacation?

✔ Will you provide the proper vaccinations and yearly veterinary checkups?

✔ Will you spay or neuter the cat?

✔ Are you able and willing to keep the cat indoors to prolong and improve the quality of her life?

✔ Are you willing to clean litter boxes, give medication, clean up messes, groom, clip claws, and do all the things necessary to keep Callie healthy and happy?

✔ Will you patiently teach your cat all the things she needs to know to be a well-behaved member of the family?

✔ Will you forgive her if she scratches the furniture, breaks a few of your possessions, or coughs up a hair ball on your carpet?

✔ Will you never raise your hand in anger toward her?

✔ Are you aware that you are responsible and legally liable for your cat's actions, and are you willing to accept that responsibility?

✔ Are the other people in the household supportive in your desire to have a cat?

✔ If you rent, are you allowed to have a cat?

✔ Will your other animal companions get along with her?

✔ Will you provide supervision to the children in the household, teach them how to care for the cat, and make sure they do not mistreat her?

✔ Will you still love your Rex when she grows up? If you are not looking forward to your cat's adult years, please don't buy a Rex or any kind of cat.

Pet, Breeder, or Show?

Pet-quality Rex are the most affordable. They are purebred and can be registered with any cat association that recognizes the breed. However, in the breeder's estimation, they will not be suitable for cat show competition because of cosmetic flaws of coat, conformation, or color. Pet quality does not mean the cats are not healthy or will not make fine companions. Unless you are a judge or breeder, you may not be able to tell the difference between pet and show quality. The cosmetic faults can be very subtle.

Breeder-quality Rex have good potential for producing quality offspring. A Rex breeder may sell breeder-quality cats for slightly less than show-quality cats.

Show-quality Rex are assessed by the breeder to be outstanding examples of the breed, and they should do well in competition. (Remember, though, that buying show-quality cats does not ensure that your cats will win at shows.) Show-quality cats are the most expensive. Some breeders also sell "top show-quality" Rex. This means the breeder believes the cats can make finals consistently after they have achieved grand champion status and are good enough to compete for high regional or national awards. If you are interested in a show-quality Rex, wait until the kitten is at least six months old to buy her. The kitten's show prospects can be judged more easily if you wait until the kitten is out of the lanky teenager period. Too, some Rex go through an ugly-duckling period or periods of molting. These are normal but will affect your ability to judge the cat's merits.

If you want a Rex for a companion and you have little or no interest in showing, buy pet quality. A pet-quality Rex will make as good a companion as the finest grand champion and will cost considerably less. Too, pet quality will be much easier to obtain. Since the Rex breeds are rare and the kittens are in high demand, getting a show-quality Rex may be hard or impossible unless you are a seasoned exhibitor.

Read the breed standard, talk to breeders, and take in a few cat shows before starting the selection process so you'll know what you are looking for. It occurs rarely, but some disreputable people represent their cats as show quality when they know their cats are not worthy of that classification. On the other hand, if a

---

TIP

Choosing a Kitten

A healthy kitten's eyes are bright, clear, and do not run. The face should not have tear stains. Her nose should be damp and cool to the touch. The kitten should not sneeze or wheeze, and her nose should not run. This could be a sign of respiratory illness.

In the male, the space between the anus and the genital opening is greater than in the female. The female's genital opening looks like a small slit, while the male's sexual orifice is round.

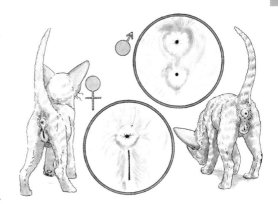

breeder or dealer is selling Rex for much less than average, be wary. Discounted Rex are risky business and may have genetic defects, health concerns, or behavior problems. Be an informed consumer. Never buy a Rex that has no papers or that cannot be registered with the cat associations. This is a sure sign that something is wrong.

Male or Female?

Since you will be altering the cat when he or she is old enough, gender really doesn't matter. Either male or female will make fine companions.

By the time the kittens are ready to go home with you (12 to 16 weeks), telling a male from a female will be easy. Lift the kitten's tail, and look at its rear end. The female's genital opening is directly below the anus and looks like a small slit. With the male, the anus and the penis are spaced farther apart, and both openings are round.

Adult or Kitten?

While kittens are loads of fun, getting an adult Rex is sometimes better and often less expensive. By missing the kitten stage, you also miss the most destructive stage of Callie's life. Too, if you have a limited amount of time (and don't we all?), an adult will often require less time initially in terms of training and care. The Cornish, Devon, and LaPerm are active, playful, and retain their playfulness well into adult-

hood, so you will not be missing out completely by getting an adult.

Too, you can often get an adult Rex for less than you would pay for a kitten. Breeders will sometimes have adult Rex that have been bred or shown and are now ready to retire. They may also occasionally have adult cats that didn't turn out to be as promising in the shows as expected. Sometimes breeders will place these retired breeder or show cats into good homes for around the cost of a pet-quality Rex and sometimes less. Some breeders will even place retirees for the nominal cost of vaccinations and spaying or neutering, but this depends upon the breeder and the demand for the breed.

Indoors or Out?

One of the controversial issues regarding domestic cats in North America today is whether to keep cats indoors or allow them to roam freely. Some cat lovers feel that keeping cats inside is cruel. They feel cats should not be denied the opportunity to enjoy the fresh air, sunshine, and diversion the great outdoors provides. They feel the trade-off is worth the risk—a short, stimulating life is better than a long, less exciting one.

Other cat lovers feel that subjecting cats to the hazards that the outdoor life provides is irresponsible. Personally, I share this view; keeping companion cats indoors is responsible and prudent. Cats are not wild animals and do not have the necessary skills to survive outdoors, particularly in these hazardous times. When you consider all the dangers to which Callie is exposed, there really is no justification for allowing her to roam. An indoor cat can live 15 years, sometimes even 20. An outdoor cat, on average, will not celebrate her tenth birthday. The Rex, with her curiosity and high activity level as well as her rarity and value, is particularly vulnerable to outdoor hazards. If keeping your Rex indoors is not an option, consider buying a different kind of pet.

One Cat or Two?

Of course, indoor cats do need companionship and entertainment, so consider how much of the day Callie will spend alone. Cats are social animals and need company and attention. If you will be away from home all day, consider getting two cats so they can be company for each other while you are out earning the cat food. A single, indoor-only cat, alone all day and deprived of feline company, can suffer from loneliness and may become depressed, as we do when we are kept from the company of our family and friends.

Choosing a Kitten

Look for a kitten that is healthy, happy, and alert. A healthy kitten is curious and playful. Her fur is clean and soft. Look at the fur's roots. If you see tiny black particles clinging to the hairs, she has fleas.

A healthy kitten's eyes are bright, clear, and do not run. The face should not have tear stains. Her nose should be damp and cool to the touch. The kitten should not sneeze or wheeze, and her nose should not run. This could be a sign of respiratory illness.

The kitten's ears should be clean and free of dark-colored wax. She should not shake her head or scratch at her ears. Doing so indicates infection or ear mites. Her anus should be free of fecal matter or evidence of diarrhea.

Gently pry open the kitten's mouth. A healthy kitten's gums and mouth are pink with no sign of inflammation. The teeth are clean and white.

A 12-week-old kitten should have her first and second shots, and her fecal exam should show her to be free of internal parasites. Ask for a copy of her veterinary records when you buy the kitten.

Cornish Rex are active, social cats that enjoy the company of feline friends.

A kitten's temperament is equally important. Observe the litter for a few minutes. Tempt the kittens with a cat toy, and see how they react. You'll notice some kittens are bold, while others prefer to hang back and check out the action from a safe distance. Look for a kitten that seems curious, friendly, intelligent, and used to handling. Don't choose a kitten that cowers from your hand, runs away in terror, hisses, snarls, or struggles wildly. Avoid kittens that appear overly passive or unresponsive. This could be a sign of health problems as well as temperament concerns.

Cats are individuals; they behave according to their unique natures. In any given litter you will notice a range of behaviors. However, one reason for buying a purebred is that she will take after her parents in conformation, coat, and personality. The kitten will exhibit some Rex behavior.

If all the kittens seem unaccustomed to human contact (provided they are more than six weeks old), find another breeder. Kittens with little early human contact are less likely to form strong, trusting bonds with their humans.

The Sales Contract

Most breeders have conditions under which they sell their cats. Read the contract carefully. If you have questions or concerns about the conditions, ask the breeder for clarification. If you think the conditions are unreasonable or too restrictive, buy from another breeder. Once you sign the contract, you are legally and morally obliged to honor it.

Breeder contracts vary. Common issues addressed include declawing, breeding, spaying and neutering, and the cat's care, housing, diet, and medical treatment. Some contracts require you to keep the cat indoors and to give the breeder an opportunity to buy the cat back if you can no longer keep it. Many contracts prohibit the cat from being sold or given to pet shops, shelters, or research laboratories.

It is also a common practice for breeders to withhold a cat's papers until the new owners provide proof of alteration. This is reasonable, given the cat overpopulation problem. Breeders also want to keep the quality of their Rex breed high. That means preventing less-than-perfect cats from being bred by people who may not know much about breeding.

Spend some time with prospective kittens before making your choice. Take your time and avoid buying on impulse.

Finding a Rex breeder is fairly easy, even though the Rex breeds are less common than others. Buy one of the magazines listed in the back and check the breeder listings. You can also find breeders through the Internet; see "Useful Web Sites" in the back. Try to find one in your area.

If the breeder has no Rex available, he or she may recommend another breeder who does. Or ask the breeder to inform you when kittens are available. Sometimes you can put down a deposit. However, if possible, see the kitten personally before agreeing to buy.

Cat magazines also have listings of upcoming cat shows. Attending a cat show is a great way to meet breeders and see their cats. Breeders who produce cats that meet the breed standard will likely also show their cats. You usually will not find breeders at cat shows who produce poor quality cats. At such shows their cats are subject to scrutiny by experienced judges, exhibitors, and breeders who can quickly spot a bad apple, so cat shows are usually good places to meet and talk with reputable breeders.

Contact a cat association-affiliated Rex breed society; they can provide member lists and these organizations usually have a written code of ethics the members agree to uphold. The cat associations may also provide lists of breeders (see page 92).

Call breeders on weekday evenings, before nine P.M., please. On weekends breeders are often away at cat shows. Prepare a list of questions before calling. A caring breeder will be willing to answer all questions. If the breeder lives far away, ask to see photos. Many breeders have web sites where you can see photos of their cats; be sure to ask. Call the cat association or society to which he or she belongs to check a breeder's credentials before committing to buy.

Don't be surprised if the breeder asks you questions as well. Some of these questions may seem rather personal, but try not to take offense. Responsible breeders are attached to their cats, and want to make sure they go to loving, trustworthy homes. In fact, a breeder who seems eager to sell to just anybody could be a bad risk. If the breeder isn't concerned about finding good homes for the kittens, how much care do you think he or she put into breeding the kittens in the first place?

Look for a cattery where the kittens are raised "under foot," meaning the kittens had the run of the house and plenty of the human interaction vital to proper socialization.

BREEDER

Questions You Should Ask

First, ask how the kittens are raised. You want a kitten raised underfoot in a loving home environment, rather than in an isolated cattery with little human contact. Also ask if you can see both of the parents, or only the mother. By seeing the parents, you'll have a better idea of the adult appearance and temperament of the offspring.

Ask the breeder to provide names and phone numbers of people with whom he or she has previously placed cats. Ask these Rex owners about their experiences with the breeder. Of course, a breeder is likely to provide only the numbers of people who have had positive experiences.

Ask whether a veterinarian has examined the kittens, what vaccinations have been given, and if the kittens have been tested for feline leukemia (FeLV) and feline immune deficiency virus (FIV). Ask if the breeder guarantees the kitten against genetic or health problems. Responsible breeders should be willing to stand behind their cats.

Ask in which cat association(s) the breeder's cats are registered. This is important if you decide to show the cat, because each cat association has different show standards and rules regarding the Rex breed.

If you decide to buy from this breeder, ask him or her what cat food he or she recommends. If you wish to change foods when you bring the kitten home, gradually switch from the old food to prevent stomach upset or diarrhea.

Visiting the Cattery

If possible, choose a breeder whose cattery you can visit, because then you can see how

To properly pick up your Rex, put one hand under the front legs, and scoop up the cat with the other hand by pushing under its rear quarters.

the kittens have been raised. Most breeders operate their catteries out of their homes.

When visiting the cattery, let your eyes and nose be your guides. Does the place smell clean, or does it reek of urine and feces? Does the cattery look tidy and well cared for? Are the cats comfortable around people, or do they slink around and hide? Are toys, scratching posts, and other cat items in evidence, or do you get the impression the breeder views cats as just a moneymaking venture?

Often you'll have to wait before picking up your Rex. Responsible breeders do not release their kittens until they are at least 12 weeks old, and some hold onto their kittens for 16 weeks or longer. It's vital to a kitten's development that she spend the first weeks of life with her mother, so don't begrudge the kitten the extra time.

ACCLIMATION AND DAILY LIFE

Before your Rex arrives, make a few simple preparations. First and most important, cat-proof the house (see page 54). Second, get the equipment necessary to make Curly feel at home and to provide for his comfort and safety.

Preparing for Arrival

The following materials will provide a solid foundation for your new cat's home environment:

Cat carrier: Buy a stout plastic carrier with adequate ventilation. Many plastic carriers have reinforced wire doors allowing Curly to see out and air to get in. Wicker or wooden carriers are also available, but the plastic ones are easier to clean if Curly has an accident. For frequent feline flyers, buy a carrier made to fit under the plane's seat.

Cat bed: Many kinds of cat beds are available, so buy a cat bed that suits your taste and pocketbook. Make sure, however, that the bed and its cover are washable.

Litter box: The proper litter box is important, particularly since Curly will be kept indoors. If Curly is a kitten, you'll need a litter box shallow enough that he can step into easily (about 3 inches [7.5 cm]). As he grows, buy a deeper pan (up to 6 inches [15 cm]), to help prevent him from scratching litter out of the

Black Devon Rex.

pan. Many types of cat boxes are available. They range from simple (a plastic pan) to elaborate (electric self-cleaning devices). You may have to experiment to see what Curly likes.

Litter: Many kinds exist. The appropriate kind depends on a number of factors; ask your breeder or veterinarian for advice. Some Rex have definite opinions about the litter they prefer. Therefore, if one litter is not a hit with your Rex buddy, try another.

Dishes: Cat dishes are available at pet supply stores, or you can use dishes designed for humans. These are often cheaper, but make sure they are free of lead-based glazes. Lead can leech into food and water and may poison a cat. Heavy, shallow ceramic bowls are a good choice. Avoid plastic dishes because they can contribute to feline acne.

Scratching equipment: If no scratching post is available, Curly will satisfy his natural desire to scratch by shredding the couch, chairs, or carpets. Scratching equipment comes in a variety of styles, shapes, and price ranges, so let your pocketbook be your guide. The post must have a sturdy base so it will not tip over and frighten Curly into scratching elsewhere. Carpeting usually is not a feline's favorite scratching material, so try a cat post with sisal fiber rope or natural bark.

Cat toys: Rex tend to like interactive toys in which you play an active role. Avoid toys with an attached string unless all play is supervised and the toys put away when finished. Otherwise, Curly could wind the string around his neck, creating a choking hazard.

Cat-proofing Your Home

Before you bring home your Rex buddy, take some time to cat-proof your home. Cats are, for the most part, smart and savvy survivors, but a few precautions will make your Rex safer and ease your mind.

Kitchen appliances: Keep dishwashers, freezers, refrigerators, ovens, and microwaves closed when not in use. Rex are particularly interested in appliances used to store food. Unplug appliances like blenders, toasters, elec-

tric kettles, irons, hot plates, and so on, when you're finished with them. Supervise stove tops when they are in use.

Garbage and trash cans: Keep them covered, particularly cans used to dispose of bones and other food wastes. If your cat swallows these, they could be harmful or, in some cases, fatal.

Cupboards and drawers: Rex cats, with their dexterous paws and curious natures, can learn to open cupboards and drawers. Secure them with childproof latches if they hold hazardous materials such as bleach, disinfectants, solvents, cleaners (particularly those containing phenol), insect sprays, and ant, mouse, or rat poisons. Cats have a poor ability to detoxify their systems, so even small amounts of toxic substances can kill.

Bathroom cabinets: Secure the medicine cabinet with childproof latches. Cats can be poisoned by some common medications that are safe for humans such as aspirin and acetaminophen (found in brands such as Tylenol). One Tylenol tablet can kill a cat. Keep pills and vitamins safely in their bottles, with lids secure, until you are ready to take them.

Bathroom appliances: Unplug hair dryers, curling irons, electric razors, electric toothbrushes, and anything else with a cord when not in use.

Toilets: Keep the lid down if you use chemicals in the tank to keep the bowl clean. Cats drink out of toilets just like dogs do, and toilet bowl cleaners can be poisonous.

What's wrong with this picture? Rex are known for their curiosity and dexterity. It's important to protect them from household hazards.

Laundry room: Dryers should be kept closed; many cats have been killed in dryers. Warm, clean clothes attract cats and your Rex may crawl into this nice warm cave for a nap.

Living and family room: Put breakables and valuables you can't live without into display cases or out of reach, or secure them so they cannot be knocked over. Rex can be rambunctious and active. Screen fireplaces and heaters. Use candles, kerosene and oil lamps, and other fire sources only when you can supervise them.

Electrical outlets and cords: Cover exposed electrical cords, or disconnect them when they are not in use. Particularly when young, cats sometimes chew on electrical wiring and can be seriously burned or electrocuted. The chewed wiring can also start fires. Even if Curly does not have a spraying problem, seal unused electrical outlets with protective plastic inserts available at hardware stores.

Craft/hobby supplies: Unplug hot-glue guns, soldering irons, and sewing machines. Store any potentially toxic material (paints, glues, varnish) in a secure area. Put away sewing and craft supplies when not in use. Cats are particularly attracted to string, thread, yarn, and other sewing supplies. Death can result from swallowing stringlike items if the string lacerates the intestinal walls.

Windows and balconies: Screen all windows that will be opened. This is particularly important if you live above the first floor, but you don't want Curly escaping anyway. Balconies should be off-limits; some cats do not have a good sense of height and may fall.

Houseplants: Indoor cats may eat poisonous varieties because of the limited availability of eatable greens. Because cats like to nibble greenery, provide Curly with a safe substitute such as oat or wheat grass. These can be easily grown or purchased at pet supply stores, health food stores, and some supermarkets.

Bringing Curly Home

When you are ready to pick up your new Rex, schedule a veterinary appointment for examination and testing. This exam is particularly important if you already have cats at home; you don't want to expose them to contagious diseases. To be on the safe side, get the examination before allowing Curly to mingle with his new companions, and keep him in isolation for at least two weeks.

Pick up Curly when you can spend time together, such as just before the weekend. When you arrive home, set the carrier in a quiet place, and allow Curly to get used to the new sights and smells. At first he will feel vulnerable and uncertain. When he calms, Curly will be curious about his new home. When you think he is ready, let him out of the carrier. Allow him to explore, giving him as much quiet time as he needs to feel comfortable. You will feel tempted to handle Curly at this point, but restrain yourself. He needs to feel in control of this new, frightening situation. If you have other cats or pets, keep them away for now.

When he has completely explored the room, allow him to settle down and gain confidence before you allow him into the rest of the house. Offer him food, water, and his litter box, allow him to sleep if he wishes, and give him plenty of love and attention. Introduce him to his bed, scratching post, toys, and dishes. At this stage, do not hold or restrain your Rex unnecessarily; wait until he becomes more accustomed to you.

Kittens and Kids

Children as well as adults feel the need for an animal friend, one that loves them unconditionally and is always there for them. Caring for a cat companion can be a great way for children to learn responsibility and compassion.

However, teach your children that cats are living creatures with feelings of their own. Teach them how to handle cats properly. A kitten's rib cage is very soft, and rough treatment can cause fractures and internal injuries. Rough handling can also cause the cat to bite or scratch in self-defense.

When Curly arrives, enlist your children's cooperation in helping him adapt to his new home by having them sit quietly beside the carrier. That will allow your children to feel involved in the cat's socialization while allowing Curly time to calm down. When you let Curly out, have your children keep an eye on him as he explores his new environment, but do not let them interfere with the cat's explorations. If you encourage your children to participate in your cat's daily care and grooming as well as in the cat's playtime, they will form a close bond of friendship with Curly that will last throughout his life. They also will learn to respect the other animals that share our planet.

Handling Your Rex

Some Rex allow you to hold them on their backs, but most do not like it much. In general, active, energetic cats like to have their toes pointed down when they are held. Your Rex will let you know what he prefers. If he wiggles, cries, or looks unhappy, try a different position. If he puts back his ears, hisses, or threatens to scratch or bite, put him down at once. Never pick up a cat or kitten by the scruff of the neck; this can cause serious harm. Mother cats pick up their kittens by the scruff, but you shouldn't try it. Leave scruff carrying to the experts. However, holding a cat *down* by grasping the scruff, particularly when you are restraining one that feels angry or frightened, is OK.

The Importance of Play

Even adult cats need to play, and playing will bring Curly and you closer. I am not talking about flinging a cat toy into the middle of the room and expecting Curly to entertain himself while you go fix dinner. Where is the challenge in attacking a limp, lifeless hunk of fabric? I am talking about interactive play that will help cement the human/feline bond.

When holding a Rex, support the rear legs with one hand and the chest area with the other.

Keeping Curly indoors is definitely good for his health. Provide play sessions to keep your indoor Rex stimulated and active.

Play helps keep Curly mentally and physically active. It also provides an outlet for his energy, so he is less likely to act aggressively or develop behavior problems. Play also helps defuse the tension in multicat households. It also burns calories, maintains muscle tone, and improves circulation. Obesity is a growing problem for pets, and an exercise program is as good for Curly as it is for you.

Play relieves boredom, particularly for indoor-only cats. If left alone, an indoor cat can become bored, lonely, and depressed. Interactive play helps alleviate these feelings and can stimulate the release of endorphins, giving the cat a sense of well-being and self-esteem.

Playing with your Rex benefits you, too. Researchers are discovering that people who regularly spend time touching and playing with their pets have lower cholesterol levels,

Cornish Rex kitten. Regular play sessions will keep your Rex healthy and happy.

lower blood pressure, a greater chance of survival after surgery, and less depression and anxiety.

Bonding with Your Rex

Cultivating a friendship with Curly takes time and effort. First you must establish trust. How long this process takes and how successful you will be depends on a number of factors. Cats

are individuals, and no two will react exactly the same way. While Rex cats are generally devoted and affectionate, their personalities depend greatly on their upbringing and their early experiences with humans. In general, you'll have better success bonding and training a cat that has been well socialized early in life.

In developing a bond with Curly, remember four things:

Consistency: If you allow Curly to walk around on the dinner table one day and whack him for doing the same thing the next, he will be bewildered. If given enough inconsistent treatment, Curly's self-confidence will be damaged. He will become uncertain and anxious around you, not knowing how he is expected to behave. Showing Curly that you can be counted upon to behave consistently and fairly will help him trust you.

Affection: Cats are extremely sensitive and perceptive animals. They can sense your moods and emotions. Studies suggest they are able to tell who likes them and who does not merely by observing subtle physical signals such as tension, eye contact, and odors. You will have better luck establishing a bond with a cat you genuinely like.

Kindness: Cats love and obey people who treat them well. Show Curly he can rely on you to behave acceptably. This means not holding him when he does not wish to be held (except, of course, during necessary duties such as claw clipping, pilling, and bathing); never hitting, shoving, kicking, or throwing him; speaking softly to him; and providing him with love, attention, and entertainment.

Patience: You may want Curly to sit on your lap. However, picking him up and holding him there before he is ready for that level of close-ness will alienate him rather than build your bond. Don't force yourself on your cat; allow him to set the pace of your relationship. Each cat has his own level of comfort with human interaction. Give him the time he needs to get to know and trust you, and your bond will last a lifetime.

Your Aging Rex

As cats age, their bodies go through changes. Cats are considered seniors at around ten years of age. At first, the signs of aging are not obvious. Perhaps Curly begins to sleep more, becomes less playful, exhibits behavioral changes, and gains or loses weight. As he ages, he becomes less active and more susceptible to certain diseases and illnesses. His metabolic rate may decrease. He may become less agile, less flexible, and his eyesight and hearing may become less acute. For this reason, Curly's litter box, food dishes, and bedding should be put in easily accessible places. You should consult your veterinarian to make sure Curly is getting the nutrition he needs. He may need a more energy-dense food or one with fewer calories (see page 61). Too, some older cats need special diets to help ease the burden on the kidneys or liver. Your veterinarian is best able to make these determinations.

Old cats are also more susceptible to heat and cold, and this is particularly true of the sparsely furred Rex breeds like the Devon and the Cornish. Keep the house at a consistent, comfortable temperature. Senior cats may spend less time grooming, causing the coat to look greasy or unkempt. Obese cats or cats with arthritis or joint disorders may also have diffi-culty grooming themselves and so will need grooming from you. These changes are a normal part of aging.

Be alert for the following symptoms as Curly ages since they can mean serious disorders:

✔ Excessive drinking and frequent urination (possible signs of diabetes or kidney problems)

✔ Lumps under the skin (tumors)

✔ Hyperactivity, wakefulness, thirst, diarrhea, and increased appetite accompanied by weight loss (hyperthyroidism)

✔ Bad breath, drooling, and pain when eating (tooth decay, gingivitis)

✔ Stiff or painful movement (arthritis)

✔ Weight loss (liver or kidney failure)

✔ Lack of appetite, frequent vomiting, and diarrhea that may contain blood (pancreatitis)

✔ Difficulty breathing, coughing, shortness of breath, abdominal distention, weight gain, and reduced tolerance to exercise (heart disease)

✔ Straining to urinate, blood in the urine, and passing small amounts of urine (feline lower urinary tract disease).

Personality changes may occur as well. Curly may be more easily irritated and less tolerant of environmental changes. Just as people do, cats become set in their ways. Changes in Curly's daily routine or in his environment upset him. Even moving his favorite sleeping pillow to a new location can upset an aging Rex. For this reason, avoid introducing new pets or subjecting your senior cat to rough handling and loud noises. The less household commotion around the aging Rex, the better he will be able to cope.

The senior cat may forget his litter box training because of increased urination or bladder or gastrointestinal problems. When your cat begins showing signs of aging, reinforce his toilet training to head off problems before they begin.

All of us get old, if we live long enough. Treat the senior Rex as you would want to be treated—with gentleness, respect, and love.

Euthanasia

Euthanasia is a humane way of ending an animal's life. At some point you may have to consider euthanasia, even if your Rex is not old. It is often the most difficult decision an animal lover makes. However, consider Curly's quality of life over the sadness you will feel at his death. If your cat is in constant pain that cannot be relieved, if he is terminally ill and has no chance of recovering, if the treatment for his disease is not likely to succeed and means great suffering, then perhaps the time has come to let your friend go.

The veterinarian can arrange for disposition or you can handle the arrangements yourself. You can choose cremation or burial. Pet cemeteries are available in many areas, or in some areas you can simply find a quiet place in your yard for your Rex's final resting place. Check with local authorities to see if that is allowed in your area.

If the veterinarian suggests an autopsy would benefit cat medical research, consider allowing him or her to do the procedure. It may make you feel better to know your cat's death benefited future feline welfare.

The intensity of your grief may surprise you. Your sorrow may last a few weeks or much longer. In many areas, pet grief support groups and support hot lines are available to help you through this period. Ask your veterinarian or local humane society. Don't feel silly for mourning. Curly is not just an animal—he is a loved family member.

Proper nutrition is vital if your Rex is to live a long and healthy life. Dietary needs vary depending upon your cat's age, health, activity level, and metabolic rate.

Since most Rex are active cats (the exception is the Selkirk Rex, which is more placid in temperament), their nutritional needs are usually greater than, say, the more sedentary Persian. Because they are active, Rex also tend to have hearty appetites. You are liable to catch Callie diving headfirst into your plate at mealtimes or, if she knows better than that, reaching up a long, agile paw to snag a bit of your dinner when you're not looking.

Because we now know so much about feline nutrition and because manufacturing cat food is a multibillion dollar industry, you have myriad choices in kitty fare. If armed with some basic information, you will easily find foods that will match your pocketbook, give you the convenience you desire, and the nutrition Callie needs.

Types of Cat Food

Three types are available: dry, semimoist, and canned. Each comes in a variety of flavors, and each has advantages and disadvantages.

Dry foods: These consist of animal protein meals, cereals, corn and soy meal, and supple-

Longhaired red Selkirk Rex.

ments formed into small, crunchy, fat-covered nuggets. Dry food is inexpensive and easy to store since it does not go bad as quickly as canned or semimoist foods. Unlike canned foods, dry cat food can be left out for your cat to nibble throughout the day, convenient if you are not around to feed Callie when she's hungry. The chewing action can also play a role in reducing tartar buildup on the cat's teeth, and that helps maintain healthy teeth and gums.

Semimoist foods: These usually come in foil-lined bags or in single-serving pouches. They have a higher moisture content than dry foods but are produced in much the same way and have much the same ingredients. They have some of the same advantages, too. They are easy to store and feed, can be left out longer without spoiling, are lower in cost than canned foods, and lack the odor canned foods can have. However, semimoist foods will not help reduce tartar as dry foods may.

Canned foods: Although more expensive than the other two and not as easy to feed, canned foods are highly digestible, usually higher in protein, and Callie may like them better than dry or semimoist, making them good choices for finicky eaters. Canned foods are about 75 percent water and are a good source for cats that need a higher fluid intake, such as those with kidney disease. They are also good for cats with sore gums or that have lost teeth to dental disease since they require almost no chewing. Cover and refrigerate leftover canned food. Be sure to warm the leftovers to room temperature or slightly higher before you offer them to Callie—cats will usually not eat refrigerated foods. They like their food to be around body temperature.

Premium, Popular, and Economy Brands

In addition to choosing between dry, semimoist, and canned foods, you will also need to choose between premium, popular, and economy brands. Generic brands are often, but not always, lower in quality, using poorer grade ingredients and whatever ingredients are inexpensive at manufacturing time. These poorer ingredients are less digestible and may provide lower-quality protein. The cat would need to eat more to get the same amount of food value as a popular or premium brand. This can mean that the food may end up costing you more than a popular brand because the cat must eat more to get the same nutritional value.

However, some generic foods are made by the same manufacturers as the popular brands and sometimes are the same formula. However, you cannot count on this. Before choosing to feed your cat an economy brand, research the manufacturer and the ingredients the manufacturer uses.

Popular brands are nationally advertised name-brand foods and are more expensive than generic brands but less expensive than premium brands. These foods are made by manufacturers that research their products well, do testing using the Association of American Feed Control Officials (AAFCO) procedures, and meet most of or exceed the nutritional guidelines set down by the AAFCO. Too, they generally use better-quality, more easily digestible ingredients than the generic brands and provide good nutritional value.

Premium brands generally contain high-quality, more easily digestible ingredients and use an unchanging formula, unlike the popular brands that may change their formulas depending upon current market availability and cost. These foods tend to be very well researched and energy dense, so a cat needs to eat less to get the nutrition she needs. Of course, you pay more for these foods—they are the highest in price other than therapeutic diets available through your veterinarian that address certain medical conditions.

However, the pet food industry has no regulated definition of the terms *premium* and *super-premium*. Therefore, premium food manufacturers are not required to provide higher nutritional value than popular food manufacturers. In fact, some premium foods may differ little from popular brands.

Stage of Life Feeding

In the early days of cat food, cats were fed the same formula from womb to tomb. Now that more research has been done, cats' nutritional needs are better understood. Therefore, pet food manufacturers have changed the way they formulate their kitty fare. Since nutritional needs change as the cat ages, the foods available to your cat vary according to the cat's age and stage of life. Cat food is labeled according to the following stages:

All life stages: These cat foods are formulated as "one size fits all" meals. They are tailored to meet the nutritional needs of kittens, adult cats, pregnant cats, and seniors. For the food to be labeled for all life stages, the manufacturer must make sure the food meets the nutritional requirements of each life stage. Unlike a food formulated for adult maintenance, a food for all life stages will have a higher protein content, be more calorie dense, and have other nutrients added. For a healthy cat, one of these foods is usually fine. However, if your cat has a weight problem, kidney disease, or other condition, a food for adult maintenance may be a better choice.

Kittens: Because they are busy growing, kittens need more protein. A Rex kitten should receive a food that's 30 to 40 percent protein and about 17 percent fat for the first 12 months of life. Kitten food is formulated to provide those nutrients. Kittens not given the proper nutrition can develop health problems later in life, so choose a food that's labeled "formulated for growth." Dry kitten foods are generally formed into small nuggets just right for little mouths.

Pregnant or nursing cats: Pregnant queens require about 25 percent more protein than adult cats. The energy needs of lactating (nursing) queens are two to four times higher than for nonpregnant adult cats. Feed a pregnant or lactating Rex a high-protein food labeled "for growth and reproduction."

Adult maintenance: Foods labeled for adult maintenance are formulated to provide the nutrition needed by fully grown, adult cats

that are not pregnant or lactating. These foods are fine for nonbreeding adult cats. The label usually reads something like: "Kitty Krunchies Cat Food provides complete and balanced nutrition for maintenance."

The senior years: Senior cats are usually less active and have a lower rate of metabolism. Even highly active Rex slow down with age, and therefore their energy needs are less. Too, cats' bodies can become less efficient at processing food and digesting nutrients. That explains generally why cats begin to lose weight as they age. Such cats may do better on a high-quality, calorie-dense, highly digestible food. However, some senior cats develop kidney disease. A high-protein cat food is not an appropriate choice for such cats because of the strain the extra protein puts on the kidneys. On the other hand, some Rex tend toward obesity as they get older and may need a lower-calorie diet (see "Obesity," page 67).

Some pet manufacturers make foods formulated for senior cats and often label them something like: "For cats eight years of age and older." However, just like people, cats age at different rates, depending upon a number

---

TIP

Food for Seniors

You should consult your veterinarian when your cat reaches the senior years. You need to make sure she is getting the proper food for her age, health, and activity level.

Devon Rex are enthusiastic eaters, so take steps to keep Callie trim.

A Cornish Rex begging for treats. If you feed Callie from the dinner table, you'll never have a peaceful meal again.

of factors including heredity, health, breed, and lifestyle. No one senior food is going to be appropriate for all cats over a certain age.

The AAFCO and National Research Council do not have recommendations for senior diets as they do for the other life stages. Therefore, most senior diets are formulated according to the adult maintenance nutritional guidelines. What sets senior diets apart from other adult maintenance foods is the calorie content and certain ingredients like fiber. Although senior formulas vary depending upon the manufacturer,

most senior foods include less fat, more fiber, and less protein.

Unless Callie has a health concern that would benefit by a food lower in protein, a lower protein content may not be in Callie's best interest, given the way some older cats lose their ability to derive nutrients from their food. Too, low-calorie diets generally are less palatable than adult maintenance foods. You may find Callie reluctant to eat these foods, particularly if you switch the food suddenly. Since loss of appetite can be a problem in older cats, this may aggravate the problem.

Reading Cat Food Labels

Like human food companies, pet food manufacturers are legally required to supply nutri-

Shorthaired Black Selkirk Rex.

A Black Smoke and White Cornish Rex.

Since Cornish are particularly fond of food, make an effort to keep Callie from becoming pudgy in her later years.

tional information on the label. The rules governing pet food labels are based on model pet food regulations set by the AAFCO to ensure compliance with federal and state feed regulations. The label must disclose the following:

Guaranteed analysis: This specifies the minimum amounts of protein and fat and the maximum amounts of fiber and moisture. The analysis may also list maximums and minimums of ash, magnesium, and taurine, among other nutrients. The word *crude* when applied to the protein, fat, and fiber percentages describes the method used to determine the percentage, not the ingredient quality. A crude

percentage is an estimate, which means the figures given do not tell you exactly how much protein, fat, fiber, and water are in the food.

Ingredients list: This list must disclose all the items used in the food. Just as in human foods, the ingredients are listed in decreasing order by weight. You get an indication of the amount of any item by where it appears in the order. Therefore, to determine how much animal protein your cat is getting, see where meat products fall in the ingredients list. However, this can be tricky. Say the first item on the list is chicken, leading you to think that

Cornish Rex. Exercise can help keep off those extra pounds.

the food is mostly chicken. However, the next items are ground yellow corn, brewer's rice, soybean meal, and corn gluten meal. The total of these ingredients makes plant material the principal ingredient.

Statement of nutritional adequacy: This tells you whether or not the food provides complete and balanced nutrition for Callie and for what life stage(s). The label will say something like, "Animal feeding tests using AAFCO procedures substantiate that this food provides complete and balanced nutrition for all life stages." Such a statement would mean the food is formulated to meet the requirements of kittens, pregnant and lactating queens, and adult cats needing maintenance diets.

When examining this statement on your brand of cat food, note whether or not the words "complete and balanced" appear, whether the food has undergone feeding tests, and for what life stage the food is designed. You want a food that has been test fed to cats with the procedures established by AAFCO and that guarantees complete nutrition for your cat's current life stage.

Feeding instructions: Most cat food labels provide feeding instructions. The instructions might say something like: "Daily ration for an average adult cat is one 3-ounce can per 3 pounds of body weight." It might instead say, "A 6- to 10-pound cat should be fed ½ to ¾ cup daily."

Diet Changes

Provide Callie with a variety of foods so that she doesn't develop into a finicky feeder. Variety is good for her health, too. It is wise to provide the nutrients she needs from a variety of sources.

However, any change in diet should be made slowly so Callie can adjust to the new food without going on a hunger strike. While some cats can survive for weeks without food, it's dangerous to allow your Rex to stop eating suddenly, as cats will do rather than eat a food they do not like. A life-threatening condition called fatty liver disease can develop after only a few days of fasting. That explains why you should discuss any change in eating habits with your veterinarian.

Add a small amount of the new food into the cat's regular diet. Slowly over the next week or two increase the amount of the new food and decrease the amount of the old food. Callie is more likely to accept the switch that way and will have less chance of gastrointestinal upset from the new food.

Foods to Avoid

Never feed Callie raw meat, fish, or eggs. Some cat owners assume that since cats in the wild eat their prey raw, raw meat is more healthy for cats. However, muscle meats do not provide a balanced diet for Callie, and feeding raw meat may expose her to disease-causing organisms and parasites. For example, raw meat can transmit toxoplasma tissue cysts, which can lead to the disease toxoplasmosis, a disease that can be transmitted to humans. Raw eggs, chicken, and meat can carry the salmonella bacteria, which can cause a wide range of illnesses. *Escherichia coli*, a common and dangerous species of bacteria, can be found in undercooked and raw meats and other foods. Raw meat can also contain parasites such as *Trichinella spiralis*, which causes the disease trichinosis, and roundworm larvae. Any potential benefit raw foods might give your cat is outweighed by the dangers.

Avoid giving Callie milk. Mother's milk is the only milk kittens need, and adult cats do not need it at all. Also, many adult cats are lactose sensitive or lactose intolerant, which can cause diarrhea, flatulence, and other digestive upsets.

Obesity

Veterinary experts consider obesity to be the number one nutritional disorder among cats and dogs in North America today. Just as with humans, obesity can put pets at higher risk of health problems such as arthritis, joint disorders, diabetes, and heart disease. If Callie should require surgery, the anesthesia and surgical risks are greater when she is overweight. Callie's life span and overall health are impacted by excess weight, so you should work to keep Callie fit and trim.

The Cornish and Devon Rex, with their very short, thin coats, show their weight gains more readily than some breeds. They don't have all that hair to hide added pounds. You'll be able to spot Callie's weight fluctuations more easily. With the Selkirk and the LaPerm, particularly longhairs, weight gains may not be as obvious. So you will need to keep a sharper eye on these breeds to make sure Callie isn't hiding excess pounds under her curls. Feel her ribs. An overweight cat's ribs are difficult or impossible to feel. The abdomen may protrude, and fat may hang down below the belly. The cat may also develop bulges of fat on the rump, and the face may become broader.

As with humans, keeping off those added pounds is much easier than shedding them once they are on. Monitor Callie's weight, and make sure she gets a veterinary checkup at least once a year. A 1-pound (0.5-kg) weight gain may not seem like a lot to you, but for a 10-pound (5-kg) cat, it is a significant gain. Feed Callie a balanced, healthy, sensible diet, and avoid giving her too many treats. If you notice her gaining weight, take steps to take off the added weight immediately.

Obese cats (cats exceeding their optimum body weight by 15 percent) should receive a diet designed to help them lose weight. Several kinds and flavors of reduced-calorie foods are available. Consult your veterinarian for advice. To prevent your furry feline companion from going on a hunger strike, wean Callie slowly from her old food to the new one. Extra playtime with your cat's favorite toy also helps Callie stay slim and alert.

Always see your veterinarian before putting your cat on a diet. He or she will check to make sure your Rex doesn't have other health problems that contribute to her obesity. Never put an obese Rex on a strict, extremely low-calorie diet. This can cause life-threatening problems.

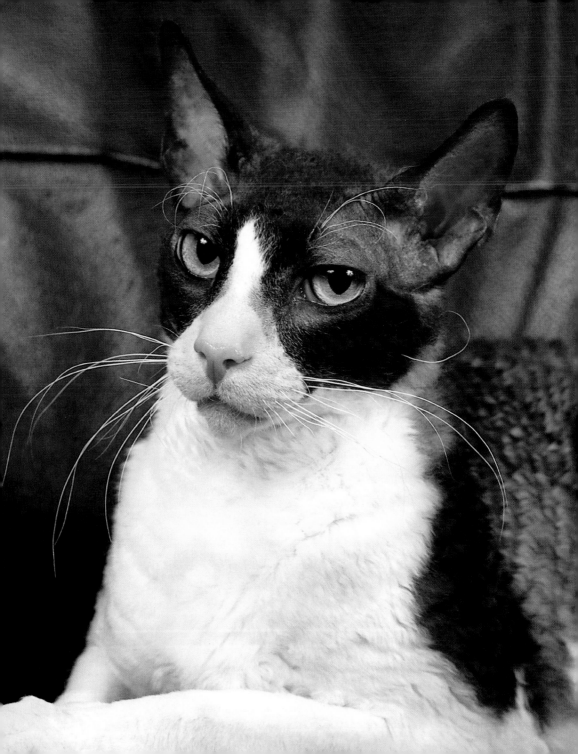

UNDERSTANDING REX CATS

In sheer numbers, cats outnumber dogs as pets in the United States today. Their strength of personality and self-confidence, along with their grace, beauty, clean ways, and affectionate natures, make them a popular choice for many animal lovers.

They are also one of the least understood companion animals, and this can cause any number of problems between owner and cat. A good understanding of the way cats think, and why they think that way, will help you have a more positive relationship with your cat.

The Cat's Senses

To be able to have an affectionate relationship with Curly, you first must have an understanding of how he perceives the world around him. Curly uses his five senses to gather data about the environment and transmit these data to the brain where they are processed into usable information.

Hearing

Since the cat has survived millennia by hunting prey animals, the sense of hearing is very important to its survival. Curly's hearing is ultra-

Black and white bicolor Cornish Rex.

sensitive—not only can he hear sounds too faint for our ears, he can also hear sounds higher in pitch than we can perceive. His hearing is tuned to a higher frequency, because the sounds of his prey—rodents, small mammals, and birds—are usually high pitched.

Not only is Curly's hearing acute, his ears are equipped with more than a dozen muscles that enable them to swivel 180 degrees toward the source of sounds. This aural arrangement helps funnel the sounds into the ear and also makes it easier to locate the source of sounds extremely accurately. So when you see Curly sitting with his back to you but ears furled backward, this means that although he appears to be ignoring you, he is keeping an ear on your movements.

Sight

The feline's sense of sight is highly developed and allows him to see in almost total darkness as well as in the brightest sunlight. Although cats cannot, as you may have heard, see in total darkness, Curly's eyes use the available light much more efficiently than do ours. This is in part due to the *tapetum lucidum,* a reflective layer of cells that lines the back of the retina. This "mirror of the eye" reflects unused light back through the retina, giving the light-sensitive retinal cells a second chance to use the light.

Because their corneas are relatively larger and more curved than ours, the cat's total field of vision is wider than ours—285 degrees to our 210 degrees. When Curly is looking directly ahead, he can see movement in any direction except directly behind him. This wide area of peripheral vision is highly tuned to movement. So even when Curly apparently doesn't notice you, he is likely very much aware of your presence.

Touch

The sense of touch provides Curly with vital information regarding pressure, warmth, cold, and pain. This information is transmitted to the brain where it is processed so Curly can take the proper action—crawling out from under his heavy littermate, moving away from a too-hot fire, finding a warm place to sleep, and fleeing when you step on his tail.

Curly's whiskers, touch-sensitive vibrissae, are important touch receptors. The slightest whisker movement stimulates a network of nerves and provides detailed information about the cat's environment. This is vital to Curly's ability to move about at night with confidence, and navigate through thick bushes and through cluttered barns and storerooms virtually by feel.

Smell and Taste

Although the dog's olfactory sense is far better than the cat's (and worlds better than ours), cats have a finely tuned sense of smell that they use not only to gather information but also as a means of communication. Cats use their senses of smell and taste, as well as their senses of hearing and sight, to perceive and define their environment. With our weak sense of smell, we can only imagine the rich world of aromas perceived by our feline companions.

Smell and its companion sense of taste team up to become a sensory system known as the chemical senses. Smell and taste organs are closely linked. Both senses are registered in the same part of the brain, and the nasal passage opens into the mouth.

Cats have a sense we lack that is best described as a cross between taste and smell. This sense is governed by the vomeronasal organ situated between the nose and the palate and connected to the roof of the mouth by a duct. When a cat smells something interesting, he opens his mouth in a distinctive, slack-jawed grimace called the flehmen response that brings odors into contact with the organ. The organ gathers chemical molecules from the odors and transmits the data directly to the brain.

Indoor Cats

Cats are territorial by nature. Their society is structured in a dominance-controlled hierarchy governed by strict rules of conduct. Indoor cats do not lose their territorial nature. However, the territorial boundaries in multicat homes are usually small and can vary depending upon the time of day. Members of an indoor-only clan usually arrange themselves into a more or less amiable hierarchy. One dominant cat is in charge, and all the rest of the cats share middle rank. Favorite sleeping spots, furniture, the rug by the fire, or even a sunny spot by the window can be claimed

Cats mark their territory by spraying urine onto vertical surfaces. Altering usually eliminates this behavior.

by the dominant cat. The other cats lay claim to other areas they can feel is theirs alone. However, these areas may change depending on the time of day. Many indoor cats have time-share arrangements on favored spots; this behavior is very common in multicat households. All cats need at least one spot to call their own, however, and overcrowding is as upsetting to cats as it is to humans.

For example, a spot by the window might be a favored spot while the sun is warming the carpet underneath and is claimed by the dominant cat. When the sun moves on, so does the dominant cat. The other cats may now spend time by the window without fear of being rebuked by their dominant housemate.

Olfactory Language

If you have ever owned a cat, you know how much cats depend upon their sense of smell. Any new object, creature, or person brought into the home, and any change in his environment, will provoke Curly to investigate with his nose immediately. Since cats are territorial animals, they pay close attention to their environment, and even minor changes can be stressful. Even small changes in our households, trivial to us, can bring an enormous flood of olfactory stimuli to a cat.

Cats mark their territory with scent. Rubbing is the most common form of marking, although cats use scent marking in several ways to define their property. Cats have scent glands on the temples, the upper lip, the gape of the mouth, the chin, the footpads, and the root of the tail;

around the eyes; and in the anal region. These glands produce secretions. When Curly rubs up against objects, he leaves his scent so he and other cats can identify his property. These secretions give cats a wealth of personal information.

When Curly scratches the cat tree—or the new couch—he is also marking his territory. Scent glands on the underside of the paws leave personal markers on the scratched item, and the scratches serve as visual markers as well. It also removes dead nail from the claws.

Cats also use urine and feces as scent markers. The least pleasant form of scent marking (to us) is spraying, and this behavior has caused plenty of friction between humans and cats. Cats, particularly unaltered males, will spray urine to mark territory. Curly backs up to a vertical surface such as your new couch, raises his tail, and sprays urine onto the surface. He is not being bad or spiteful when he does this, although cats have been known to use elimination as a form of human behavior modification. He is merely marking his territory. Even with our weak sense of smell, the intact male cat's urine smells

Cornish Rex. When all is not right in his cat kingdom, your Rex will make sure you know his feelings on the subject.

tion mark shape. His ears are upright and perky, his pupils are neither constricted nor dilated, and his whiskers are spread and relaxed. A cat approaching you in this manner means he feels happy to see you. Other clear signs of affection are purring, kneading, rubbing, head butting, and slow blinking. You will learn to recognize these signs of affection as you get to know Curly and develop a close relationship with him.

Cats will avoid fighting when they can. They use a variety of body postures to signal their intentions. Most standoffs end peacefully after a stare down; the cats glare balefully at each other until the weaker of the two gives in and moves away. The standoff may or may not be accompanied by an exchange of swipes with their paws and growling or hissing. Usually, the stare is all they need to communicate the dispute.

If the defensive cat cannot or will not retreat or if he feels cornered or trapped, then a fight can occur. A frightened, defensive cat faced with a stronger opponent assumes one of two body postures. He arches his back, turns his body sideways in relation to his attacker, bends his tail into an upside-down U, and bristles his fur to give the impression of size and ferociousness. Alternately, he crouches low, tail held close to the ground, ready to strike out if necessary. By

terrible (the male cat has one of the strongest-smelling urines in the animal kingdom, and that says a lot). Fortunately, neutering usually curbs this behavior. However, spraying can also be a sign a cat feels anxious or threatened. Even neutered males and spayed females have been known to spray if they are having a territorial dispute with another cat or are experiencing a disturbance in their routine.

Body Language

A cat uses a variety of body postures to show his affection for humans and for other animals. A friendly, confident cat walks with his tail held high. The tip of the tail sometimes curves slightly to form a furry ques-

The four basic body language postures, from left: happy and content, aggressive, frightened, and defensive.

Devon Rex. Make sure your Rex has the proper scratching equipment to keep him from clawing the couch.

assuming these postures, he is warning his opponent to back off. Unlike dogs that roll on their backs to signal submission to dominant members of their species, cats don't have a submissive posture. When a cat rolls onto his back, he is freeing up all four feet to defend himself.

An aggressive, angry cat, on the other hand, presses the attack. He sidles up stiffly, staring at his opponent, pupils constricted, tail swishing, movements tense and slow. His ears are twitched to the side to detect attacks from the rear and side. As aggression increases and the aggressive cat attacks, the ears swivel and flatten to prevent damage.

Vocal Language

Cats use a variety of meows, murmurs, yowls, and screams to communicate with other cats and with their humans. You can interpret these as greetings, demands, pleas, complaints, or challenges, depending on the tone. As you get acquainted with your feline friend, you will become familiar with his individual vocabulary and know when he wants to eat, play, be petted, or just be left alone to sleep in the sun.

Purring

Purring is one of the most recognized feline sounds. Cats purr when they are contented, when pleased to see their human or cat friends, and when hungry. Female cats also purr when they are

courting and mating. Cats can apparently purr at will; it's not an involuntary response to emotion.

Cats also purr when they are in distress. The distress purr occurs when a cat is in a stressful situation and needs comforting. Cats have been known to purr when ill, in labor, frightened, or even dying. Cat behaviorists now believe cats can purr in response to any strong emotion.

Growling and Hissing

All cats, wild and domestic, growl as a warning. Although cats occasionally growl playfully as

Litter Training

Location, just like in real estate, is important to successful litter box training. If Curly doesn't like where the litter box sits, he may avoid it. Put the litter box into an area that allows privacy but is convenient for cleaning.

dogs do, the body language accompanying the growl indicates whether Curly is sincerely angry. The sound can range from a low grumble to an open-mouthed growl that shows he feels threatened and is ready to take offense. Growling can progress to full-scale screams of rage or fear if the threatening encroacher doesn't retreat.

When threatened, irritated, or angry, cats expel air sharply through their mouths in a distinctive sound called hissing. Spitting is similar to hissing; however, it has a sharper and more explosive sound. Although cats sometimes hiss playfully, they usually make these sounds when they become angry. It means, "Leave me alone!" or "Back off!"

Scratching Problems

Cats have a natural need to scratch. Watching Curly use the new couch as a scratching post is frustrating. Rather than punish him, however, give him substitutes to scratch upon and teach him to use them. When Curly begins scratching at a forbidden spot, say "*No!*" and put him onto his post or pad. When he uses the post correctly, praise him and give him a treat. Curly will get the idea.

Cats also scratch out of boredom. Providing Curly with toys and diversions will help. Keeping a cat's nails clipped helps, too (see page 80).

If your Rex continues scratching in inappropriate places, try rubbing the post with catnip to make it more appealing. Make the problem areas less attractive by putting double-sided tape or aluminum foil on the floor below the scratched area.

Tape inflated balloons to the problem areas. When a cat pops one with his claws, he will avoid scratching there again. However, try this only when you are home so you can pick up the balloon pieces before Curly eats them.

Sometimes, you can resolve scratching post avoidance by moving the post to a new location. Your Rex may not like the location (if, for example, another cat has claimed the area). By moving the post, you provide Curly with options.

Declawing

Declawing domestic cats to prevent scratching problems is controversial. Some countries, such as Britain and Germany, have outlawed the practice as barbaric and unnecessary. Many United States breeders, veterinarians, cat registries, and cat associations feel the same way.

Declawing removes the germinal cells and some or all of the terminal bone in the toe, similar to cutting off a human's fingers at the first joint. Usually only the front claws are removed, since they cause the most damage to furniture and possessions. The surgery requires general anesthesia, and the cat is subject to the risks anesthesia entails.

Declawing removes a cat's ability to defend himself and to climb to avoid attackers; therefore declawed cats must be kept inside. Too, some cat owners say they noticed personality

Declawing removes the terminal bone of the claw and the claw tip.

changes in their cats after the surgery, including failure to use the litter box appropriately and increased aggression due to the cat's inability to defend himself.

In recent years, pet stores have been selling soft vinyl caps that can be applied over Curly's trimmed nails and held in place with adhesive, effectively blunting the claws and making damage to belongings impossible. The caps last until the nail grows out, about four to six weeks, and then are reapplied. Your veterinarian applies the first set and provides training in their application. From then on, you can do the application at home. Usage can be stopped whenever you wish. This is a positive, painless, and safe alternative to declawing. See your veterinarian for more information.

Litter Box Problems

Litter box avoidance is one of the most frequent feline behavior problems. Inappropriate urination or defecation means a cat is trying to tell you something; cats use elimination as communication (a kind of e-mail, if you will). A new pet or person, a move or change in schedule, overcrowding, or a conflict with another cat can cause a cat to avoid the box.

If Curly urinates or defecates outside the box, schedule an appointment with the veterinarian. Urinary tract infections can cause inappropriate urination. If the veterinarian rules out a physical problem, take a look at what is going on in the cat's life. Recognizing the reasons for litter box avoidance will help you find a solution.

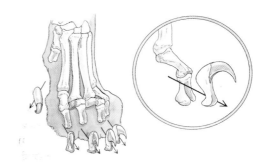

A common reason for litter box avoidance is the cat's natural cleanliness. A dirty litter box can make Curly turn up his nose and look for a private corner to do his business. Try changing the litter more often. Once a week is usually sufficient, but some cats are not comfortable with that. Scoop the solid wastes and soiled litter daily. Some cats don't like sharing their litter box with other cats; provide one box for each. The size, shape, and depth can also affect Curly's behavior. Try another size or type.

If a problem occurs after switching brands of litter, try changing back. Some litters are highly perfumed and are offensive to some cats. Other litters just do not have the right feel. Experiment with various litters, or try mixing several kinds. Just do not mix clumping and nonclumping litters.

Punishing a cat will not solve litter box problems. That will only teach Curly to eliminate when you're not around. Since cats locate their litter box by scent, rubbing his nose into the urine will only teach him that this is a good spot to urinate. Addressing the problem's cause will end the unacceptable behavior. Ask your veterinarian or breeder for advice if you're stumped for a solution. Medications exist that can help persistent problems.

GROOMING YOUR REX

Even though cats are naturally clean animals, most cats need some help from their human companions to keep looking sharp. Preferably, you should begin a grooming program as soon as Callie has settled into her new home.

Caring for the Rex Coat

Grooming can be a pleasant experience for both of you if she is trained to tolerate grooming when she is young. She will come to expect and even enjoy her grooming sessions with her preferred person.

A regular grooming program is also good for a cat's health. Grooming removes dead hair that can form hair balls in a cat's stomach (as well as covering your couch), gets rid of dead skin and dander, stimulates the skin, tones muscles, and encourages blood circulation. It is also a good opportunity to examine Callie for developing health problems and attend to them in their early stages (see page 87).

Grooming the Cornish Rex

One might expect a very shorthaired cat to need little or no grooming, but that is not necessarily the case with the Cornish Rex. Some Cornish Rex require bathing to keep them clean

Even with their short coats, Cornish Rex require some grooming.

because of the buildup of oily sebaceous secretions. These secretions are normal and all cats produce them. Cornish Rex just do not have as much hair to absorb the secretions. If allowed to accumulate, these secretions can cause skin problems and may make the coat look greasy. Weekly cleaning of the coat with special cat shampoo or a tearless shampoo does the trick (see below). Since the Cornish's ultrashort coat dries quickly, Callie will not have to spend all day putting her coat back in order as an ordinary cat would.

Grooming the Devon Rex

Devons need very little grooming. Their favorite grooming tool is your hand, applied onto their heads and down their backs. Because they lack guard hairs, Devons shed less than other breeds. Their short, wavy fur is quite fragile and brittle. Excessive brushing can actually cause hair breakage. Because the hair is fragile, the Devon can develop bald patches that remain until the next hair growth cycle, which usually occurs in fall and spring.

Like the Cornish, regular bathing is recommended since a buildup of oils can occur. Bathing is generally easy since Devons are usually easy to handle and their coats are wash-and-wear. Drying time is minimal since the hair is so sparse and short. A quick pat dry and a sunny window are really all you need. Ear cleaning once a week or so is also recommended since Devons tend to get a waxy buildup in their ears (see page 80).

Grooming the LaPerm

Unlike the Devon and Cornish coats, LaPerms come in longhaired and shorthaired versions, so the grooming needs vary depending upon hair length. In the shorthaired LaPerm, the coat is soft and wavy over the shoulders, back, and undersides. In the longhaired variety, the hair is medium long and the curls range from tight ringlets to long corkscrew curls.

However, LaPerms are generally low-maintenance cats. Even the longhairs need less grooming than most other longhairs to keep looking sharp because the silky coat does not mat easily. LaPerms lack the downy undercoat that causes mats to form in the coat. A good combing once or twice a week for shorthairs and two or three times a week for longhairs will keep the coat free of loose hairs. Like all cats, LaPerms shed. According to fanciers, though, they do not shed as much as cats with normal hair. Still, regular combing not only keeps the coat free of dead hairs but also reduces the amount of cat hair covering your furniture.

LaPerms have wash-and-wear hair. Managing the coat's curliness is easy—a bath and towel drying sets the curl. When completely dry, spritz the fur with water since this tends to add more curl to the coat. Blow-drying makes the hair frizzy and is not recommended for this breed.

Grooming the Selkirk Rex

The Selkirk's hair is longer than that of the Devon and the Cornish, and Selkirks shed just like any cat. They do require grooming, although their fur does not mat as easily as one might expect. Like the LaPerm, the Selkirk's coat comes in both shorthaired and longhaired versions, so the grooming needs depend upon hair length. The shorthaired coat is medium in length and arranged in loose, individual curls. A good combing once or twice a week will keep the shorthaired Selkirk in good shape.

The longhaired Selkirk has long, wavy hair that is longer than a Maine Coon's though not as long as a Persian's. However, grooming the longhaired Selkirk is not too difficult since the coat lacks the light, flyaway fur that would cause it to mat easily. A good combing two to three times a week removes dead hairs and prevents matting.

Bathing makes the fur curl up to its best advantage, so monthly bathing is recommended. Be sure to comb out the coat before bathing. Combing after the bath will straighten the coat and take out the curl. Therefore, owners usually pat the coat dry and leave it alone to finish the drying process. Spritz the coat with a spray bottle full of water after bathing to enhance the curl. High humidity can also affect the amount of curl in the hair, just as it does with curly human hair. After patting the coat dry, blow-dry the coat for best results.

Hold Callie on your lap and press the pad of the foot gently to extend the claws. Clip the white area of the nail.

Claw Clipping

Callie will need her toenails trimmed about every two to three weeks. Not only does this save on the wear and tear of your furniture, it reduces the risk of your cat injuring you, your family, and your other pets.

Use nail clippers designed for cats, available at any pet supply store. With Callie held in your lap, hold one paw and *gently* apply pressure on the paw to make the claws extend. Clip off the white part of the nail, being careful not to cut into the pink quick. The quick is rich with nerve endings and hurts very badly if cut—probably akin to getting a sliver rammed under your fingernail. Do not cut the white part of the nail any closer than a tenth of an inch (2.5 mm) from the quick. If you hurt Callie while clipping her nails, she will not react well to having her nails clipped from then on. If you have never trimmed a cat's nails, you may want to ask your veterinarian to show you how.

A cat can injure you quite severely, so heed Callie's body language when you clip her nails. If she reacts badly to having her nails clipped, which some cats do, enlist help to get the job done. Have your partner hold Callie down on a sturdy table or other firm surface. Trim the front claws first. When you get to the back feet, have your partner hold Callie on her side

Be careful not to cut into the pink quick; this is very painful and will make Callie reluctant to have her claws clipped in the future.

so you can reach the back feet. Be careful—she may try to rake you.

If your cat goes completely insane at the idea of claw clipping and cannot be handled, try catching her just after she has awakened from her afternoon nap and is sleepy, and do one or two nails each time. If this doesn't help, or if she runs under the bed when she sees you coming, you might have to enlist the help of your veterinarian to get the clipping done.

Hair Ball Prevention

While the Devon and the Cornish do not have much of a problem with hair balls, due to having less hair, they can still get hair balls. The Selkirk and the LaPerm do need a hair ball preventative, particularly the longhairs. Every week for longhairs, every other week for shorthairs, treat your kitty to a dose of a petrolatum

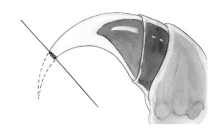

product such as Petromalt. For the Devon and Cornish, once a month is usually enough unless Callie has a problem with hair balls. Read the directions on the tube for the exact amount to give.

To administer, smear a dab onto your finger and see if Callie will lick it off. Some cats like the taste since it is flavored with malt. If Callie turns up her nose, smear a dab onto her paw and allow her to lick it off. (Avoid using this method within a week of a show, however.) Callie swallows less fur while licking it off if you dispense the preventative after her grooming session. Smear it on well to prevent your cat from shaking the stuff off all over your carpet. Use only as directed—too much can hinder the absorption of fat-soluble vitamins.

Routine Ear, Eye, Face, and Nail Care

The area around the eyes (particularly under the eyes) can accumulate dirt, dried tears, and

Keeping your Cornish Rex's claws clipped will also make her less likely to snag your clothes or scratch your skin.

sleep residue. During the grooming session, or whenever Callie seems to need a bit of extra attention, wipe the eyes clean with a cotton ball moistened with warm (not hot) water. If the under-eye area develops stains, use a tear stain remover available at your local pet supply store.

The ears of the Rex breeds, particularly the Devon and Cornish Rex, often need more

Longhaired brown tabby Selkirk Rex. Bathing makes the Selkirk's fur curl up to its best advantage. Spritzing the coat with a spray water bottle will enhance the curl.

Black and white bicolor Cornish Rex.
Make nail care part of your Rex's
grooming routine.

attention than those of an ordinary cat. The amount of waxy buildup varies from cat to cat. In general, though, the ears of most Devon and Cornish cats will need regular attention to keep them free of excessive waxy discharge. Look inside the ear flap. If you see dark accumulations of wax, Callie's ears need to be cleaned. If your Rex accumulates wax quickly, plan on a once-a-week cleaning. Good-quality feline ear-cleaning solutions can be purchased at some of the larger pet supply stores or through mail-order pet supply catalogs; ask your breeder for a recommendation.

While using a cotton swab or cotton ball dipped in ear-cleaning solution, carefully clean the waxy buildup from the inner ear area. Be careful not to poke the swab or any object into the ear canal, because you can cause severe damage to the ear. A good idea is to ask the breeder for an ear-cleaning demonstration before you take Callie home. If you cannot meet with the breeder because your cat was shipped to you, ask your veterinarian to show you how.

The nails may also need cleaning. Cornish and Devon Rex tend to accumulate wax around the nail beds and between the toes. These areas should be cleaned of waxy buildup often, because the wax will cause the nails to collect dirt, bits of cat litter, and other debris. Use a cotton ball or swab dipped in the ear-cleaning solution to clean the nails and between the toes.

Because of the waxy buildup, some Rex will get blackheads on their chins. Regular cleaning of the area will reduce the problem. Some

breeders use a dry shampoo powder to absorb oils and clean the chin and paws. These are worked into the fur and then brushed out with a soft facial brush. Liquid waterless shampoos are also available; these are sprayed on, massaged into a lather, and toweled off. No rinsing is needed. Others use facial cleansers intended to clean human skin. These cleansers are generally massaged onto the chin fur and then rinsed out. Be sure to check with your veterinarian to make sure the product is safe for cats, however. What is safe for humans is not necessarily safe for cats, and cats readily absorb toxins through their skin.

To keep your Rex from accumulating oily deposits, regular bathing is recommended, particularly for the Cornish and Devon Rex. Too, if Callie has chronic problems with parasites or skin allergies or does not properly attend to her grooming, regular bathing certainly benefits her health. Pregnancy, obesity, and advancing years can also make proper grooming difficult. Longhaired Selkirks and LaPerms can have trouble keeping clean after a trip to the litter box.

Routine bathing of your cat may benefit your health as well. Recent studies have shown that regular bathing of cats can remove a good percentage of the allergenic pro-

tein secreted via saliva and sebaceous glands that trigger allergic reactions in humans. Wiping Callie down daily with a sponge and distilled water helps wash off the saliva she has licked onto her coat and also may help reduce allergic reactions.

Many veterinarians recommend bathing Callie in a kitchen sink equipped with a spray hose attachment, because you have more control over her when you're standing up. You can buy a rubber spray hose attachment inexpensively at a bath or hardware supply store. If your sink is too small or Callie too big, use the tub. Whatever you choose, be sure you can close off the area. Chasing a

wet, soapy Rex over the sofa and under the bed is not much fun.

Before bathing Callie, trim her nails. Giving blood is admirable only when you are donating to the local blood bank. Then comb the fur thoroughly. This is important for longhaired Selkirk Rex and LaPerms. As the coat dries, mats tighten against the skin so they are almost impossible to remove; they then must be cut out with scissors.

Assemble all the needed supplies before you begin. Some breeders recommend using a degreasing dish soap on Devon and Cornish Rex to help remove the accumulation of oils. Be aware that these soaps can dry Callie's skin. Never use flea shampoo designed for dogs. The concentration of insecticide in dog shampoo can be harmful or even fatal to cats.

Put Callie into the sink with her back facing you so she will not scratch you if she strikes out or struggles. Hold her in place by applying gentle pressure to the shoulders. If Callie becomes uncontrollable, grip her by the nape and push down, being careful not to push her head under water, which will cause her to

Keep your Rex's back toward you so if Callie strikes out, she'll be less likely to scratch you.

panic. Gripping the nape usually makes the cat freeze. Remain calm, and never yell at or strike your cat—that frightens her further. A panicked cat can seriously injure you. Talk soothingly; she needs reassurance. Never spray the head, face, or ears, and never dunk a cat's head under water.

When Callie is completely wet, apply shampoo with the squeeze bottle. Work it into the coat well. Don't neglect the legs, the feet, between the toes, and the tail. Gently clean the hindquarters and the anal and genital areas with soft washcloth.

After soaping, rinse well using the spray attachment. You must get all the soap out of the fur, because Callie grooms after her bath and ingests any remaining soap. Continue rinsing until the fur has lost the slick, soapy feel and the rinse water runs clear.

After rinsing her thoroughly, run your hands down your cat's body to remove excess water. Wrap her in a terry towel with just the head showing. Since you cannot safely wash your cat's face during the bath, now is the time to use a warm, damp terry cloth washcloth to clean her head, face, and chin.

Change the towel, and dry Callie well. Pat, don't rub, the fur. Rubbing can damage the fragile Devon coat and can create tangles in the longhaired varieties of the Selkirk and LaPerm. When the coat is as dry as possible, leave Callie in the enclosed area to sulk and groom herself. Do not let her into drafty areas or outside until she is completely dry. Most

When drying Callie, pat, don't rub, your Rex's fur.

cats will groom continuously until they are dry. For the Cornish, Devon, and LaPerm, blow-drying the fur is not recommended.

The Selkirk's coat can benefit from blow-drying, however. Use the blow-dryer on the low setting only and avoid blowing directly into Callie's face or ears. Many owners use their cat carrier as a drying cage. This allows them to dry their cat without being required to hold cat and dryer. Set up the dryer to blow into the carrier, and leave Callie in the drying cage with the dryer set on the lowest setting for about 20 minutes. Never leave her unattended with the dryer turned on.

KEEPING YOUR REX HEALTHY

Choosing the right veterinarian is one of the most important decisions you will make regarding your Rex's health. You and your veterinarian will be partners in caring for Curly and protecting his health, and you will be an active participant in the process.

Choosing a Veterinarian

Your veterinarian will provide the expert medical care, diagnoses, exams, vaccinations, treatments, and medications. You will provide the daily home care that will keep your Rex healthy and happy.

Most veterinarians are highly trained medical professionals who have received as much and sometimes more education and training as human physicians receive. However, a few uncaring or unqualified individuals will have slipped through the cracks. So you need to be discriminating when choosing the right veterinarian. After all, you are trusting Curly's life to this person. Your veterinarian must be willing to spend time answering your questions and discussing your concerns.

Veterinarians who specialize in feline medicine usually have the equipment and expertise to give a cat excellent care. If such a specialist is not available in your area, a veterinarian who has ample experience in caring for small

A very healthy Cornish Rex.

domestic animals would also be a good choice. Your veterinarian should be close by and provide 24-hour emergency service or referral. Ask other cat owners, your breeder, or local humane society personnel for recommendations. Find a veterinarian who is experienced in treating Rex cats and who knows the conditions and diseases to which they are prone.

The veterinarian's office should be clean, well maintained, and free of unpleasant odors. The support staff should be knowledgeable and caring. The technicians should follow approved disinfectant techniques on equipment before and after your cat is examined. If the examination table on which you are expected to place your precious Rex is covered with cat hair and feline footprints, choose another veterinarian.

Make an appointment to talk with the veterinarian before services are needed. Write down your questions ahead of time so you will remember what you want to ask. If he or she doesn't answer your questions to your satisfaction, or if you feel uncomfortable with the veterinarian in any way, try another.

Vaccinations

The good news is that vaccinations can prevent some of the most common feline diseases. While no vaccination is 100 percent effective, vaccinations have saved countless feline lives. Make vaccination part of your Rex's basic health care.

Vaccinations introduce a modified form of the disease organism into the cat's system, causing the cat's body to develop antibodies against those organisms. This usually results in immunity. Booster vaccinations are needed because if Curly does not encounter the disease, he may lose his immunity. Boosters renew the antibody response.

Although vaccines are usually safe and adverse effects are rare, occasionally life-threatening allergic reactions can occur. Because of possible complications, only qualified veterinary personnel should administer vaccines. Any unusual symptoms noticed after vaccination should be immediately reported to your veterinarian.

Outdoor cats can be quickly exposed to disease transmitters such as parasites, wildlife, and other cats and their wastes. Even if your cat lives indoors and will not be shown or bred, some vaccinations should still be given. Many areas require that cats be vaccinated against rabies. If Curly bit someone, he could be euthanized if you could not produce a current rabies vaccine certification.

In the past, veterinary professionals recommended booster vaccinations every year, except for the rabies booster, which was given once every two to three years. In 1997, the American Association of Feline Practitioners (AAFP) and the Academy of Feline Medicine (AFM) formed an advisory panel to study the risks and benefits of vaccines. They developed new vaccination guidelines based on research indicating that the duration of immunity produced is longer than previously thought. They also studied the correlation between vaccination site sarcomas and vaccination protocol (see below).

Under these guidelines, vaccinations are divided into two categories: *core* and *noncore*. Core vaccinations, recommended for all cats, are rabies, panleukopenia (feline distemper), respiratory virus herpesvirus (which causes rhinotracheitis), and calicivirus. These diseases are severe and easily transmitted, while the vaccines are generally safe and effective. Noncore vaccinations, recommended for cats in high-risk situations, are feline leukemia virus (FeLV), feline infectious peritonitis (FIP), dermatophytosis (ringworm), and *Chlamydia psittaci.*

Vaccination Site Sarcomas

In the early 1990s, veterinarians discovered that a malignant cancer called sarcoma can form at vaccination sites. Rabies and feline leukemia virus vaccinations appear to cause sarcomas more often than other vaccines. While rare (one to three sarcomas per every 10,000 cats vaccinated), sarcomas are life threatening and the cure rate is poor.

A Vaccine-Associated Feline Sarcoma Task Force was formed to study and address this concern. This ten-member team is composed of representatives from the major veterinary associations, the United States Department of Agriculture, and the Animal Health Institute. It gathers information about sarcoma and educates veterinarians and cat owners. More information can be found on their web site: www.avma.org/vafstf/default.htm.

The task force recommends that veterinarians use a new vaccination protocol to track the problem better. Veterinarians are asked to give the rabies vaccine in the right rear leg and the leukemia vaccine in the left rear leg. Not only does this make the sarcomas easier to track, but treating a sarcoma on the leg is easier than one located between the shoulder blades.

The task force also recommends that cats be given only the vaccinations they really need and at less frequent intervals. For example, if your cat is kept indoors and has no contact with other cats, he may not need the feline leukemia virus vaccine, because his exposure to the disease is unlikely. The rabies vaccine, however, should usually be given, because many states mandate it. Rabies can be passed to humans, so the risk of the disease outweighs the risk of vaccination.

The task force recommends vaccinations; they have saved millions more lives than they have taken. If the new guidelines are followed, the benefits of vaccination outweigh Curly's risks. You and your veterinarian should decide which vaccinations are appropriate for your cat's lifestyle and at what intervals to give them.

Yearly Veterinary Checkups

Even if you do not have Curly vaccinated annually, he needs annual checkups to protect his health and help detect any developing conditions or diseases. Curly's body can undergo profound changes within a year's time. For cats ten years and older, an exam every six months is wise since cats tend to develop more health problems as they age.

A yearly exam will accomplish several things:
✔ Curly's weight will be recorded and causes of loss or gain discussed since both can be signs of underlying illness. If he is becoming

obese, your veterinarian can recommend a sensible diet for Curly.
✔ You will have the opportunity to discuss feline nutrition with your veterinarian and make sure Curly's diet is appropriate for his needs, which is particularly important as he ages.
✔ Your veterinarian will examine Curly and screen him for early signs of disease or illness. When diseases and conditions are diagnosed early, treatment is more likely to be successful and less costly. Too, more treatment options usually exist.
✔ Curly's teeth will be examined for signs of dental disease and, if present, proper treatment can be started.
✔ You can discuss behavior problems, their causes, and their treatments, including possible drug therapy. Your veterinarian may refer you to a behavioral specialist if the problem is severe and persistent.
✔ Your veterinarian can examine Curly for internal and external parasites and discuss appropriate parasite control.

Spaying and Neutering

As part of your Rex's routine health care, get him or her spayed or neutered at the appropriate time. Preventing unwanted pregnancy is the most important reason to alter, but it has behavioral and physical advantages as well. Early altering means a cat will not display the restlessness, yowling, spraying, and other sexual behaviors of intact cats. Unspayed females have a seven times greater risk of mammary cancer than neutered females. Spaying also eliminates uterine infections and the risk of ovarian and uterine cancer. Neutered males have a lower risk of certain types of cancers as well.

Longhaired tortoiseshell Selkirk Rex.

Altering will not make Curly fat and lazy. Only too much food and too little exercise will do that. Additionally, having one litter will not calm down Callie.

Neutering reduces aggressive behavior in males. One of neutering's biggest benefits, though, is the reduction of the hormone levels that prompt spraying. Neuter Curly as early as possible before these behaviors become life-long habits. The risks are small compared with the benefits.

The American Humane Association reports that between 5.9 and 9.9 million cats are euthanized in shelters each year. It is vitally important all cat owners spay and neuter their pets. Two cats and their subsequent offspring, if allowed to reproduce at will, can produce more than 150,000 kittens in only seven years. Please, be a responsible pet owner and alter your pets.

At-home Physical Exams

In addition to Curly's yearly veterinary exams, you should examine Curly each month for signs of parasites, illness, and disease. Run your hands over his entire body and tail, feeling for any swellings, lumps, growths, or abscesses. Check for tenderness, thin or bald spots, flea dirt, excessive skin flaking, and fur mats. Be sure to run your fingers over Curly's vaccination injection sites (usually between the shoulder blades or on the flanks) to detect possible injection site sarcomas.

Curly's ears and eyes need attention, too. His eyes should not have discharge and his inner eyelids (haws) should not protrude. These can be signs of serious illness. His ears should be checked for waxy buildup (see page 80). If you see excessive dark, waxy buildup that looks like coffee grounds, schedule a veterinary appointment. Curly may have ear mites.

Routine Tooth Care

Examine Curly's teeth. A healthy adult cat's teeth are white and clean. The gums are firm and pink, and they attach closely to the teeth. If a bright red line appears along the gum near the teeth, it may be a sign of gingivitis—inflammation of the gums. If left untreated, gingivitis, plaque, and tartar can undermine your cat's health and affect his kidneys, nervous system, heart, and liver. According to Tufts University School of Veterinary Medicine, periodontal disease is the most common disease of domestic cats.

Plaque is a combination of bacteria, food particles, and saliva. Plaque deposits harden onto tooth surfaces, become tartar, and enlarge the pocket between the tooth and the gum. These pockets are ideal homes for bacteria that invade the gingival tissue, causing swelling, bleeding, and pain. Eventually, the gum ulcerates, and the bone holding the tooth erodes, causing the teeth to loosen and begin to fall out. Periodontal disease is more serious than gingivitis and requires professional care. Loose teeth must be removed and the remaining teeth professionally cleaned in order for the inflammation to subside. Sometimes antibiotics are given to treat the infection. Some Rex are prone to gingivitis; be extra vigilant about Curly's dental health.

Gingivitis can be a sign that Curly is sick. Causes of gingivitis include squamous cell carcinoma (a malignant kind of tumor), viruses such as feline leukemia (FeLV) and feline calicivirus, systemic diseases such as diabetes mellitus and kidney disease, and immune disorders such as feline immune deficiency virus (FIV). If you see any signs of gingivitis, schedule an appointment with your veterinarian. He or she may advise you to make toothbrushing a part of Curly's weekly grooming. This will extend the period between veterinary teeth cleanings and reduce your expense—and the risk to Curly, too.

✔ Bleeding/abnormal discharge from a body opening
✔ Coat changes (dullness, dandruff, excessive shedding, loss of hair, bald patches)
✔ Difficult urination, inability to urinate, blood in the urine
✔ Difficulty in breathing, wheezing, choking
✔ Discolored tongue
✔ Disorientation
✔ Extreme thirst, increased water intake
✔ Increased hunger or food intake
✔ Increased urination
✔ Lumps or swellings
✔ Persistent cough
✔ Pupils different sizes or unresponsive to light
✔ Refusal to eat or drink
✔ Repeated vomiting
✔ Seizures
✔ Severe diarrhea
✔ Staggering, head tilt, inability to walk normally
✔ Sudden blindness or vision disturbances
✔ Unexplained weight loss or gain
✔ Unresponsiveness, unconsciousness, extreme languor, weakness

Serious Signs of Illness

If you see any of the following signs, take Curly to the veterinarian immediately:
✔ Abdominal pain/body held in a hunched position

Shorthair cameo Selkirk Rex.

Feline Diseases

Disease	Symptoms
Feline Infectious Peritonitis (FIP): body's immune response to the virus helps virus to spread throughout the body and cause damage.	Wet form: labored breathing, fever, listlessness, appetite and weight loss. Dry form: lethargy, weight loss, intermittent fever.
Feline Leukemia Virus (FeLV): causes tumors, attacks the growing blood cells in the bone marrow, suppresses the immune system.	Rapid weight loss, anemia, sluggishness, poor appetite, recurring colds and infections.
Feline Immune Deficiency Virus (FIV): suppresses feline's immune response. Note: similar to human HIV but cannot infect humans.	As the disease suppresses the immune system, secondary infections take hold; symptoms vary and include malaise, loss of appetite, gingivitis, weight loss, fever, recurrent infections.
Feline Panleukopenia Virus (FPV): also called feline distemper. One of the most contagious and destructive feline diseases.	Sudden fever, appetite loss, dehydration, depression, coat dullness, vomiting, painful abdomen. Infected cats often assume a hunched position.
Rabies (was called hydrophobia): virus can infect most warm-blooded animals including cats, dogs, skunks, raccoons, humans.	Behavior changes including hiding, irritation, aggression, derangement; facial paralysis, drooling.
Feline Viral Rhinotracheitis (FVR): also called rhino and feline herpes. Highly contagious; affects the respiratory system.	Sneezing, coughing, red, swollen, watery eyes; sensitivity to light; runny nose; fever; loss of appetite; depression.
Feline Caliciviruses (FCV): upper respiratory infection, milder in form than FVR.	Sneezing, coughing, red, swollen, watery eyes; sensitivity to light; runny nose; fever; loss of appetite; depression; pneumonia.
Feline Lower Urinary Tract Disease (FLUTD): group of disorders affecting the lower urinary tract. Caused by a variety of factors including bacteria, fungi, parasites, anatomic abnormalities, tumors, trauma.	Inappropriate urination, frequent voiding of small quantities of urine, blood in the urine, straining to urinate, licking urethra. In later stages of urethral blockage, depression, weakness, vomiting, collapse.

Transmission

Transmitted through bodily secretions such as feces or saliva and contaminated objects such as dishes and litter boxes. Not easily spread.

Saliva and respiratory secretions passed by mutual grooming, sharing food bowls and litter boxes, bite wounds.

Usually bite wounds; unneutered, free-roaming males at high risk. Unlike human HIV, sexual contact is not the primary means of spreading FIV.

Direct contact with infected cat's feces, urine, saliva, vomit, fleas, contaminated objects. Humans can transmit by touching infected cat or stepping into infected cat's bodily fluids.

Bite wounds are primary means of transmission.

Direct contact; shared food bowls and litter boxes; aerosol droplets from infected cat. Humans caring for infected cats can carry FVR on the hands, clothes, or feet.

Direct contact; shared food bowls and litter boxes; aerosol droplets from infected cat. Humans can carry FCV on the hands, clothes, or feet.

Two categories exist: infectious and noninfectious, but mode of transmission not known and other factors affect an episode. Note: urethral obstruction occurs much more frequently in male cats.

Treatment

FIP is often fatal; no effective treatment or cure exists. Intranasal vaccine recommended for at-risk cats.

No cure; cats can sometimes live for years with the disease. Vaccine recommended for high-risk cats; the only remedy for this killer is prevention.

No cure, no vaccine; cats can sometimes live for years with the disease. Treatment includes protecting cat from infections and treating secondary infections when they occur.

Often fatal. Vaccination recommended for all cats.

Once the clinical signs manifest, virtually 100 percent fatal. Vaccination recommended for all cats.

Often fatal, no cure. Survivors may become carriers. Antibiotics, fluids, oxygen given to treat secondary infections. Vaccination recommended for all cats.

FCV can lead to pneumonia, which can be fatal particularly to young kittens. Vaccination recommended for all cats.

Treatment varies depending upon the condition and cause. Urethral blockage is a life-threatening event and immediate medical attention is a must. Special diets may help prevent future blockages; consult your veterinarian.

American and Canadian Cat Associations

American Association of Cat Enthusiasts (AACE)
P.O. Box 213
Pine Brook, NJ 07058
(973) 335-6717
Web page: www.aaceinc.org

American Cat Association (ACA)
8101 Katherine Avenue
Panorama City, CA 91402
(818) 781-5656

American Cat Fancier's Association (ACFA)
P.O. Box 203
Point Lookout, MO 65726
(417) 334-5430
Web page: www.acfacat.com

Canadian Cat Association (CCA)
220 Advance Boulevard, Suite 101
Brampton, Ontario
Canada L6T 4J5
(905) 459-1481
Web page: www.cca-afc.com

Cat Fanciers' Association (CFA)
P.O. Box 1005
Manasquan, NJ 08736
(732) 528-9797
Web page: www.cfainc.org

Cat Fanciers' Federation (CFF)
Box 661
Gratis, OH 45330
(937) 787-9009
Web page: www.cffinc.org

The International Cat Association (TICA)
P.O. Box 2684
Harlingen, TX 78551
(956) 428-8046
Web page: www.tica.org

The Traditional Cat Association, Inc.
18509 N.E. 279th Street
Battle Ground, WA 98604-9717
(360) 687-2754
Web page: www.traditionalcats.com

United Feline Organization (UFO)
5603 16th Street W.
Bradenton, FL 34207
(941) 753-8637
Fax: (941) 753-0043
Web page: http://www.aracnet.com/~ltdltd/ufo.htm
E-mail: Uforegof@tampabay.rr.com

Miscellaneous Organizations and Agencies

American Humane Association (AHA)
63 Inverness Drive East
Englewood, CO 80112-5117
(303) 792-9900
(800) 227-4645
Web page: www.AHAfilm.org
E-mail: Link@amerhumane.org

American Society for the Prevention of
   Cruelty to Animals (ASPCA)
424 East 92nd Street
New York, NY 10128
(212) 876-7700

American Veterinary Medical Association
1931 North Meacham Road, Suite 100
Schaumburg, IL 60173
(847) 925-8070
Web page: www.avma.org

ASPCA National Animal Poison Control Center
1717 S. Philo Road, Suite #36
Urbana, IL 61802
(888) 426-4435 (to pay by credit card)
(900) 680-0000 (to have charges added to phone bill)
Web page: www.napcc.aspca.org
Note: Fee charged for crisis management

Breed-Specific Resources

Rex Breeders United
446 Itasca Court N.W.
Rochester, MN 55901
E-mail: rexbreedersunited@juno.com

The Devon Rex Breed Club
1386 Ridge Road North,
Ridge Way, Ontario
Canada L0S1N0
(905) 894-2771
Web page: http://drbc.devonrex.com

The LaPerm Society of America
808 W. Prospect Road
Ft. Collins, CO 80526

The Selkirk Rex Breed Club
P.O. Box 461
Oakland, CA 94604-0461

Useful Web Sites

Breeders' Referral List
www.breedlist.com

Devon Rex Cat Breed Directory
www.pet-net.net/devonrex.htm

Feline Advisory Bureau
www.fabcats.org/

Planet Devon
www.devonrex.com

Soft Paws Nail Caps for Cats
(800) 433-7297
www.softpaws.com

USDA Animal Welfare Information Center
www.nal.usda.gov/awic

Vaccine-Associated Feline Sarcoma Task Force
www.avma.org/aafp/default.htm

Cat Magazines

Cat Fancy
P.O. Box 6050
Mission Viejo, CA 92690
(800) 365-4421
www.catfancy.com

Catnip
Belvoir Publications, Inc.
P.O. Box 420235
Palm Coast, FL 32142
(800) 829-0926
catnip@palmcoastd.com

Cats
Primedia, Inc.
260 Madison Avenue, 8th Floor
New York, NY 10016
(917) 256-2305
www.catsmag.com

The Whole Cat Journal
P.O. Box 420235
Palm Coast, FL 32142
(800) 829-9165

Books for Additional Reading

Helgren, J. Anne. *Abyssinian Cats: A Complete Pet Owner's Manual.* Hauppauge, New York: Barron's Educational Series, Inc., 1995.
_____. *Barron's Encyclopedia of Cat Breeds.* Hauppauge, New York: Barron's Educational Series, Inc., 1997.
_____. *Communicating with Your Cat.* Hauppauge, New York: Barron's Educational Series, Inc., 1999.
_____. *Himalayan Cats: A Complete Pet Owner's Manual.* Hauppauge, New York: Barron's Educational Series, Inc., 1996.
_____ and Maggitti, Phil. *It's Showtime.* Hauppauge, New York: Barron's Educational Series, Inc., 1998.

Shorthaired Chocolate lynx point LaPerm.

About the Author

J. Anne Helgren has written six books on cats for Barron's Educational Series and is a monthly contributor to *Cats* magazine. She has written the breed profile features for *Cats* since 1992, for which she won the Cat Writers' Association Muse Medallion in 1997 and 1999 and received Certificates of Excellence in 1994, 1996, 1997, and 1999. She is a professional member of the Cat Writers' Association and the Dog Writers' Association. She has written more than two hundred articles on cats and other companion animals for national and regional publications. In addition to her writing career, Ms. Helgren teaches writing for the Long Ridge Writers' Group and serves as an editorial consultant for Barron's Educational Series, for whom she edits and critiques cat-related manuscripts and proposals.

Photo Credits

Norvia Behling: 64 (top l), 65 (top r), 68, 76, 81. Chanan Photography: 8 (bottom r), 9 (bottom l), 16 (top l, top r, bottom l), 17 (top l, top r, bottom r), 32 (bottom), 33 (top), 36 (top), 37, 40, 60, 64 (bottom), 65 (top l), 80 (bottom), 89, 93. Tara Darling: 9 (top), 12, 17 (bottom l), 57 (bottom), 64 (top r), 85. Isabelle Francais: 2–3, 5, 8 (top, bottom l), 9 (bottom r), 16, 20, 21, 28 (bottom), 29 (bottom), 32 (top), 33 (bottom), 36 (bottom), 41, 45, 52, 53, 57 (top), 61, 65 (bottom), 73, 77, 88. Gerard Lacz: 24 (top). Jorg & Petra Wegner: 28 (top).

Cover Credits

All cover photos (front, back, inside front, and inside back) by Chanan Photography.

Important Note

When you handle cats, you may sometimes get scratched or bitten. If this happens, consult a doctor immediately.

Make sure your cat receives all the necessary shots and dewormings, or serious risks to the cat's health, as well as your own, may arise. A few diseases and parasites can be transmitted to humans. If your cat shows any signs of illness, consult a veterinarian. If you are concerned about your own health, see your doctor and mention that you have a cat.

Some people have an allergic reaction to cats. If you think you might be allergic, see your doctor before you decide to get a cat.

Dedication

In memory of Goose, a very dear friend who is waiting for us at the Rainbow Bridge.

Acknowledgments

I would like to thank Grace Freedson and Bob O'Sullivan (Barron's Educational Series, Inc.) for their assistance and Amy Shojai and the Cat Writers' Association for all their help and support. I also thank Darlene Arden, Elisabeth Basore, Rebecca Rose Basore, Arlene Evans, and Betty Roby for their support and advice. Thanks also goes to Bill Helgren, my staunchest supporter and best friend. Last but certainly not least I thank Bitty, Punkin, Pooka, Goose, Clancy, Sherbert, Miss Muppet, Buddy, and all the other cats who, over the years, have helped me understand and appreciate the unique feline nature.

All inquiries should be addressed to:
Barron's Educational Series, Inc.
250 Wireless Boulevard
Hauppauge, NY 11788
http://www.barronseduc.com

International Standard Book No. 0-7641-1568-5
Library of Congress Catalog Card No. 00-064194

Library of Congress Cataloging-in-Publication Data
Helgren, J. Anne.
   Rex Cats / J. Anne Helgren.
     p. cm.
   Includes index.
   ISBN 0-7641-1568-5
   1. Rex Cat. I. Title.
SF449.R4 H46 2001
636.8'22—dc21   00-064194

Printed in Hong Kong
9 8 7 6 5 4 3 2 1